will the

REAL CHRISTIANS

please stand up?

OTHER BOOKS PUBLISHED BY BARRATT MINISTRIES:

Playing With Fire — the use and abuse of music
by Alex Robertson

An enlightening, stimulating and important book, written by a professional musician, about a much debated subject in the Church today.

FORTHCOMING TITLES PLANNED:

Radical Christianity Series, Volumes 2 and 3
by Maurice Barratt

The next volumes in this series will be an in-depth practical study of the Sermon on the Mount, following on from this introductory volume.

Manifesto for a Revolution: the kingdom of God on earth
by Alex Robertson

A study based around the parables of the kingdom in Matthew 13, bringing significant new insights as to what is happening in the church worldwide today.

will the REAL CHRISTIANS please stand up?

by

MAURICE BARRATT

Radical Christianity Series Volume 1

BARRATT MINISTRIES PUBLICATIONS
Manchester M14 5QH, England

WILL THE REAL CHRISTIANS PLEASE STAND UP?

by **Maurice Barratt**

British Library Cataloguing-in-Publication Data

A catalogue record for this book is available from the British Library

ISBN: **0 9528222 1 0**

Published 1998 by **Barratt Ministries Publications**
114 Daisy Bank Road, Victoria Park, Manchester M14 5QH, UK.
E-mail: bminmcr@aol.com

Printed by **Wright's (Sandbach) Ltd.**,
9 Old Middlewich Road, Sandbach, Cheshire CW11 1DP, UK.

CONTENTS

Part 1: The Call

Part 2: The Cost

Part 3: The Keys

Introduction

Thousands of people followed Jesus during his three years of ministry, but he was not interested in followers. He was looking for disciples — people that he could train, and teach by hidden means (parables) the secrets of the coming kingdom of God. This kingdom is within a person, and as Jesus states, it does not come with observation. It is always a condition of the heart.

When Jesus did ask people to follow him, it was always after he had told them the cost (which was to leave all, deny themselves, and take up their cross), and after they had fully understood that cost. The disciples who Jesus personally trained did understand the cost, because they left all, and in Acts chapter 6 it was claimed that these men had turned the world "upside down". This was not the boast of the apostles, but a statement from their enemies.

Our western societies contain millions of tongue-speaking evangelical Christians. They claim to have the same power of God that these early apostles had, and yet these societies are becoming more godless at an alarming rate. The church seems to have lost its power to stop this rot.

I would have no problem with this situation if the church was being persecuted. The church is God's light, and the world is certainly in darkness — incompatible with the church in every way. However, the churches seem to be in blessing, becoming more involved in the world system, and increasingly acceptable to the world.

I have been under Pentecostal evangelical teaching for forty-five years since hearing John Nelson Parr, a Pentecostal pioneer, at the age of seven, right through to the prosperity, positive affirmation, and kingdom now doctrines. But in ninety years since this Pentecostal outpouring, our societies have legalised abortion, homosexuality and witchcraft, and our governments seem to have no answers to the violence, pornography and drug abuse. These are the very things for which God judges a nation.

Surely it is time to look at our Christianity and understand that the gifts of the Holy Spirit can never make a person or people holy. It is only the **fruit** of the spirit (the character of God) that can do this and change our character from that of Adam to that of Christ. We have been developing our gifts while our fruit has been rotting. I do not believe our enemy Satan is afraid of power unless it is accompanied by character. Character is the only thing he cannot duplicate. When Jesus walked on this earth the demons cried out at his presence, but they did not say, *You are the powerful one.* They cried out, *You are the **holy** one.*

I believe there are people who are still looking for real Christianity, but where can they go to see Christians who really live the teachings of Jesus, as taught in his Sermon on the Mount? It would not be difficult in China or Cuba, where the church is being persecuted, but in the West it seems rare indeed.

There is not a shadow of doubt in my mind that true Christianity is a revolutionary process, a battle against the kingdoms of this world. I am also convinced that this battle is an internal one within a person. If we make the revolution an outward one and try to fight against and overturn the fashions, politics, commerce, and even religions of this world, then we have lost the battle for the inner man, and we may as well arm ourselves with weapons of destruction and venture off on holy wars like our misguided ancestors, the crusaders. History only proves that this is folly, counter-productive to the will of God, and a witness to the world of our godlessness. We make the same mistake the disciples made when Jesus walked this earth. They wanted a physical kingdom on earth before Jesus comes again the second time to reign as king on the earth.

That there will be physical, outward manifestations of the inner battle I have no doubt; but these outward works or acts must be consequences of the inner changes. Only when we forget our traditions, man-made doctrines and ordinances, and take a fresh, honest look at the simple and straightforward teachings of Jesus, can we see our great lack today. What a glorious thought, that we could be free from two thousand years of schism, doctrinal debates, reformations and heresies, and sit afresh at the feet of our master, simply believing and doing what he said! He is the only one who can teach us these principles; and he alone can clear the mist from our eyes.

How can I feel qualified to tackle this subject, or presume to do what many great scholars and theologians have endeavoured to do over many centuries? My only real qualification can be a personal relationship with God. Although I have spent two decades of my life studying the teachings of Jesus I realise this is not sufficient on its own. To know the book is important, but to know the author is imperative.

I have also spent the last twenty years developing a personal relationship with God, and I have learned that you cannot have a relationship with a doctrine, even a correct doctrine. Doctrines do not have emotions and feelings; God does. A doctrine can not be angry or have compassion. God, the person, does have these qualities, and this is the crucial difference. The secret to understanding God's word is understanding God.

The growth of any relationship is proportional to the time and effort spent on it. When I started to **practice** the Sermon on the Mount instead of just believing it, my life was revolutionised. It affected my work, family and everyone with whom I came into contact.

I am convinced that any open-minded person will find this book a challenge to their character, doctrines and lifestyle. I hope it will be an inspiration to let the cross work in their own lives, so that the resurrection life of Jesus may be manifested in and through them.

Part 1
The Call

Christians and the church have wanted an alliance with everything that represents power in the world. In reality this rests on the conviction that, thanks to the power of the Holy Spirit, the powers of this world have been vanquished and set in service of the gospel, the church, and mission. We must use their forces in the interest of evangelism. Wealth and various authorities receive recognition this way and are put in the church's service.

But what happens is the exact opposite. The church and mission are penetrated by the power and completely turned aside from their truth by the corruption of power. When Jesus says that his kingdom is not of this world, he says clearly what he intends to say. He does not validate any worldly kingdom (even if the ruler be a Christian). He puts us on guard against seeking any other authority than that of the Holy Spirit.

Jacques Ellul

CHAPTER 1

Calling Ourselves

The first statement I want to make about discipleship is that **we can not call ourselves**. We can decide to follow Jesus of our own free will, but we have no power or prerogative to call ourselves. Discipleship is not a "good idea".

Neither is it something that the church is obliged to practice. History has proved beyond doubt that when the church tries to produce disciples by laws and disciplines, it produces the very opposite. The Pharisees in Jesus' day were a good example of such people, following outward disciplines, rules and laws. Jesus said they did everything right according to the letter of the law, but inside they were full of uncleanness and hypocrisy.

God always works from the inside, with a change of heart, not a change of behaviour. Strangely enough, a true disciple of Jesus is not bound by outward rules and regulations at all; he is the most free person imaginable. Paul said in 1 Corinthians 6:12 that *all things are lawful* and in Titus 1:15 that *all things are pure to the pure.* This is true freedom, but it must emanate from the heart.

Let us look at Jesus' reaction to the people who offered themselves to him as disciples. You would almost think that Jesus was trying to deter them. I believe that is precisely what he did intend. In Luke 9:57 we read, *And it came to pass that as they went in the way a certain man said to Jesus, Lord, I will follow you wherever you go.*

What is wrong with this man's statement? I would suggest it is presumptuous, because he could not have possibly known where Jesus was going. Even his chosen disciples did not know this. They certainly did not expect that Jesus would die the death of a blasphemer on a Roman cross. Here is a "certain man" without a call, thinking that he could follow Jesus wherever he would go. It is not only presumptuous, it is foolish. He obviously thought that there was little or no cost, and that if there was, he would be able to handle it. Clearly, he was deceived.

Nothing's changed

The situation is much the same today with many modern followers of Christ, and I must lay the blame for this deception at the church's door. Fearing they will lose members by facing them with the full force of the challenge, it is more than they are prepared to do, and so, sadly, they produce not true disciples but their own pseudo-disciples.

What was the answer Jesus gave to this would-be disciple's offer? *Foxes have holes, and birds have nests: but the Son of man has nowhere to lay his head.*

Jesus was saying that he had nowhere to call his own, and that he had to trust other people for his food, clothes and shelter. But he was also inferring much more. Birds and foxes build their homes for more than this. Home-building is part of choosing a mate and raising a family. There is a much higher cost here than is obvious at first appearance.

In this passage of Luke there are two more examples of men who offered their services to Jesus as disciples, but in each case the answer Jesus gives is similar. We do not read that any of these three men became disciples. I fear that, like the rich young ruler, they went away sorrowful. Was Jesus being hard to these people? On the contrary, he was being most kind. He was saving them from failure and disillusionment. Consider the amazing statement that Jesus makes in Luke 14:26. *If any man come to me and hate not his father, and mother, and wife, and children, and brothers and sisters, yes, and even his own life, he* ***cannot*** *be my disciple.* This statement seems impossible to take at face value, and yet it was said not to committed disciples, but to the multitudes, maybe those who had seen the miracles and thought the lifestyle of a disciple was glamorous or easy.

Time to consider

If we accept that Jesus meant exactly what he said, then the cost of being a disciple is great indeed, and not one to be taken quickly or without considerable deliberation. Jesus simply meant that if ever there should come a situation where we had to choose between father and mother or Christ, then we are to choose Christ. We can substitute absolutely any other person or possession in this equation such as wife, children, work, church, ministry, or life itself, and the answer is always the same. It can never vary. It should now be apparent that anyone who makes this decision would be open to the accusation that they hate the person or thing that they have spurned for Christ. But this is the very term that Jesus uses. Knowing the great cost, Jesus is being considerate in his statements, because he does not want us to fail because of ignorance or misunderstanding. (If we fail because of weakness, that is a different matter entirely.)

Jesus' examples

Read carefully the two examples that Jesus now gives, of a man building a house and a king going to battle, and you will have to agree that Jesus wants anyone who is considering being a disciple to first count the cost.

Luke 14:28-32 — *Which of you intending to build a house does not sit down* ***first and count the cost,*** *to see if he has sufficient funds to complete the project, for if he completes the foundations but cannot finish the house, he becomes a laughing stock. Everyone will say that this man started to build and was not able to finish.*

Or what king, going to make war against another king, would not ***sit down first****, and consult whether he would be able with ten thousand men to fight against the enemy who has twenty thousand men? If he does not think that he can win, whilst his enemy is a great way off, he sends ambassadors and desires conditions of peace.*

Surely Jesus could not be any more explicit in his examples, or say any more to prevent his would-be followers from being disillusioned? Surely he has warned them as honestly as he can, and in the strongest terms possible? In conclusion, Jesus repeats again his opening statement in verse 33: *Just as in these two examples, whoever does not forsake all that he has, he cannot be my disciple.*

Being in the ministry, I meet many people with whom the church has failed to be honest, and they are hurt, bitter and disillusioned. In most cases they are not angry or bitter with God, but with the church and its systems. They were never told the cost, or worse still, they were told that there would be no cost and that it had all been paid for at Calvary. The price that was paid by Jesus at Calvary was for our sins, and there is nothing we can contribute to that sacrifice. But there is a price that Christians are expected to pay, and that is the cost of discipleship.

CHAPTER 2

Pierce My Ear

I believe the call to be a disciple is a personal one from Christ himself, and our decision is always a conscious one, coming only **after we have understood the cost and the consequences**. It is a decision based not on emotions or feelings, but on facts. This can never happen at the very beginning of our Christian walk, at the time when we start to follow Jesus.

It is just as absurd and unreasonable to expect that a baby could accept full time employment before it has grown, becomes strong, and understands the conditions of the employment. **I do not believe it is possible to be an instant disciple**. Discipleship is a process. Of course there are instant followers. You can make a decision to follow Jesus after your first encounter with him — but this is not discipleship.

A difficult choice

When Israel were given the opportunity to follow Moses out of Egypt, it was not a difficult decision for them to make. After four hundred years of slavery, the offer of freedom was an easy choice. They were happy to leave *in great haste*. The hard decision for Israel came after God told them to go into the promised land.

When Israel left Egypt it was with the thought of a land flowing with milk and honey. This was not a figment of their own imagination; it was God's promise to them. But what God did not tell Israel as they left Egypt was that the land was owned by giants, and they would have to fight for every inch of the ground. The cities were walled up to heaven. And we know from hindsight that an Achan in the camp meant that they would have to run from their enemies, not destroy them.

Israel's failure

It was when it came to fighting the giants that Israel failed. Paul, in his letter to the Hebrews, tells us that they refused to obey because of unbelief. Amazingly — or should we say fearfully — God did not give them a second chance, even when they repented. He told them they would die in the wilderness; and they did. Does this mean that God's plans fail if we disobey? No; it means that **we** have failed. The plan of God will never fail; but it does mean that God has to train someone else to fulfil his plan.

In fact, God broke his promise to Israel because of their disobedience. This is where the legal term "breach of promise" originates. God said in Numbers 14:34, *After the number of the days in which ye searched the land, even forty days, each day for a year, shall ye bear your iniquities, even forty years, and ye shall know my breach of promise.* It was the next generation of Israel who entered the land flowing with milk and honey, conquered the giants, possessed the land and fulfilled God's will.

Can you see the parallel in the life of a Christian? To leave the world and follow Jesus is not a difficult decision, once the scales fall from our eyes. Grace, compassion, love, forgiveness and eternal life — surely this is a promise of milk and honey. It is not a difficult decision to follow Jesus when we realise we can be free from the bondage of the world, from slavery to vice and the uncertainty of our eternal future.

Our problem comes later — when we are faced with the challenge of obedience, of taking up our cross and denying ourselves. This is often precisely where the church fails to challenge us, and instead makes it easy for us, giving us soft options and telling us that "Jesus understands", and that "this type of life appeals to only a few who are especially called".

Pierce my ear

I am going to look at a principle in the Old Testament to support my statements. In Exodus chapter 21 the first six verses are about owning a slave. The first unusual statement is in verse 2. God does not say, "you can not buy another human being", or even, "you must only buy slaves of the Gentiles and not your own people". He says, *If you buy a Hebrew servant.*

This statement may go against all our standards and moral judgements, such as the freedom of the individual and our belief that God created all men equal. But right in this opening chapter we have to decide whether we are going to simply believe and accept God's word, or change and qualify it to fit in with our traditional doctrinal thinking. We will come across this decision many times as we study the teachings of Jesus. I am going to suggest that we lay aside our own thinking and accept the simple word of God.

In fact, in God's word here in Exodus, we see that God is not against slavery, nor against the principle of buying a person. God is against bad masters, those who are cruel and abuse their power. In verse 3, God makes an important condition, that a man can only buy a slave for six years, and not for life. In the seventh year the master has to give him his freedom. In verse 16 God instituted the death penalty for the crime of **stealing** a man or woman, but this is an entirely different case from **purchasing** a man or woman.

Slavery is freedom

Let us consider the situation of the servant for a moment and forget our western mentality of rights and equal opportunities. In this period of Israel's history, poor people simply died of starvation during periods of famine or great need. To offer yourself for slavery was a way to preserve your life and that of your family. Slavery was not such a bad thing. In verse 4 there are conditions to ensure that the slave was treated fairly, and then we come across a strange statement — strange to our ears — in verse 5: *If the servant shall plainly say, I love my master.* It is strange to us because we always seem to associate slavery with cruelty and the abuse of power. The idea that someone could love his master can only mean that the master is good, and that to be his slave is actually a desirable and beneficial condition.

Consider the case of a slave with a good master. I would suggest that such a slave is actually more free than his master. Why? Because he does not have the burden of responsibility that his master does. The master supplies his food and clothing, pays the insurance, provides the accommodation and takes all responsibility for the welfare of the slave. He carries the financial burdens and all the cares that go with this responsibility. The slave is free of the financial burdens and anxieties of life.

Slaves have no rights

The only frightening thing about being a slave is that they have no rights. They cannot refuse their master. The only difficulty a slave would meet, with a good master, is one of perfect obedience. I say "difficulty", but in fact to our society it is much more than "difficult". It is completely unacceptable to even think of it, never mind to do it.

Another consideration is that slaves have no prerogative to choose their masters. The slave is up for offer. It is the master's choice. Here again we see a parallel with our own life. Read the following scriptures from John's gospel,which are all statements from the lips of Jesus himself: John 15:16, *You have not chosen me, but I have chosen you* ... John 6:44, *No man can come to me, except the Father which has sent me draw him* ... John 6:65, *No man can come to me except it were given unto him of my Father.* I can hear some readers saying at this point, "We **used** to be slaves to sin and the devil, but did not Jesus come to free us?" It is certainly true that Jesus came to destroy the works of the devil and break his hold over us — but **not so that we could be free**. We are *bought with a price* (the blood of Jesus), and we are not our own. We are redeemed from our old master, Satan, and now belong to **a new master**. Paul in 1 Corinthians 6:19 says, *What? know ye not that your body is a temple of the Holy Ghost which is in you, which* *ye have of God, and* ***ye are not your own****? For ye are bought with a price: therefore glorify God in your body, and in your spirit, which are God's.*

This sounds like slavery to me. When we follow Jesus all we do is change masters. Jesus said in Matthew 6:24, *You can only serve one of two masters.* We would perhaps feel happier if there were three choices for us to consider: God, the devil or ourselves. We like to think we have the choice of pleasing ourselves, but this is not true; in fact it is a great deception. To please ourselves is actually to serve the devil, and to love God is to hate everything else, even ourselves. We should not qualify or spiritualise the statements of Jesus, for they are simply true and to be obeyed; and obedience is the only evidence or proof that we believe.

The last verse we are considering in Exodus 21, and the last statement about slavery, is perhaps the most important principle of all. Verse 6 says this: *If the slave loves his master and does not want to go free after his six years of service, then before witnesses, his ear must be pierced through at the door-post with an awl. He must serve the same master for ever.*

Marked for life

Why does God say that the slave must remain a slave *for ever*? Why doesn't scripture say "for the next six years"? At first this seems far too binding, but if we consider it carefully, it is only reasonable. The first six years was the master's choice, not the slave's. The slave could have been left to starve. In fact, his master saved him from starvation and disaster; but now, after six years, **he can make a considered and intelligent choice** —

should he stay with his master, or should he look for another?

If you had worked for the same boss for six years you would be in a good position to know whether he was a good boss or not. You could not have known this at the interview, or even after a few weeks of employment. It takes time and familiarity for the guards and facades of our character to come down and reveal our true selves.

This is why God said the slave must be marked for life. It was to show anyone who cared to look that this man, by his own free choice, would never be free. He had the opportunity to choose freedom and decided to remain a slave. It was his own choice, and therefore it is only reasonable that it should be binding. Jesus said in Luke 9:62 that *to take up the plough of your own free will, and then to look back*, that is, to have second thoughts or a change of mind, *makes you unfit for the kingdom of God.*

Jacob

This principle is consistent throughout the bible and in all God's dealings with men. I will take just one example of many from the bible.

Jacob believed and followed the God of his fathers from his youth. There is ample evidence in the scriptures to convince us of this truth. And yet his character, as his name implies, was still that of a twister. Jacob made deals with God. In Genesis 28: 20-21 we read, *And Jacob vowed a vow, saying, **If** God will be with me, and keep me **in this way that I go**, and will give me bread to eat, and raiment to put on, so that I come again to my father's house in peace; **then** shall the Lord be my God ... and* *of all that thou shalt give me, I will surely give the tenth unto thee.*

Dealing with God

Many modern followers of Jesus have the same mentality as Jacob and make similar deals with God. They want God to bless them in the way *they* want to go, in return for their tithes and offerings. But discipleship is not about following, but about death to self and a change of character, and God eventually faced Jacob with this. Genesis 32:24-32 records that Jacob wrestled with an angel. This was his "ear piercing" experience. After this experience, his name was changed, as was his character, and he was **marked for life**. He would always walk with a limp, showing to the world that he was not his own any longer. Jacob now had the mark of God on his life.

Many Christians who fervently believe in spiritual warfare and intercession talk about Jacob and his prevailing prayer, how he wrestled with the angel and obtained power with God. This of course is to be commended; but they rarely, if ever, think of the consequences of this wrestling with God — the permanent marks it leaves on your life.

Show me a holy man and I will show you a man with Christ's marks on him. Paul says in Galatians 6:17, *From henceforth let no man trouble me: for I bear in my body the marks of the Lord Jesus.* He did not say the marks of Christ were in his soul or mind, but in his body. The marks of Christ are not always in our mortal flesh; they could be mental or spiritual marks; but they are always evident distinguishing marks in our life, and obvious to others.

CHAPTER 3

The Call of Peter

Faith is never blind. It should always be the most reasonable thing to do — not because we understand the future, or our circumstances, but because with time we have come to understand the character of God, that God is a good master who is worth serving for life; it is never an impulsive decision. It is on this basis, and only on this basis, that we make our decision. I believe that any other reason for becoming a disciple is not faith but presumption, and very dangerous.

No instant disciples

I am using Peter as an example of the fact that there is no such thing as an instant disciple. Peter may seem a strange example to use, because most people believe that Peter *was* an instant disciple — that when he was called by Jesus he immediately left all and followed him. But Jesus would not have asked that of Peter without him first following, and understanding the cost and the consequences of his decision.

Permit me to share something I have learnt over the years that I have been studying the bible. If a miracle, parable, or event appears in more than one of the gospels, then we can only find the whole truth by putting the accounts together as one whole record. The bible is inspired by God, and nothing is included by chance. Every small detail is of extreme importance. The example of Peter serves well as an illustration of this.

Peter's history

In Matthew 4:18-20 we read, *And Jesus, walking by the sea of Galilee, saw two brothers, Simon called Peter, and his brother Andrew, casting a net into the sea: for they were fishers. And He said unto them, Follow me, and I will make you fishers of men. And straightway they left their nets, and followed him.*

This narrative seems at first to be a good case for instant discipleship, but we cannot say this until we have looked at the other two gospels which record the call of Peter. In fact, we will discover that Matthew records the **conclusion** of Peter's call to be a disciple, but Luke and John gives us clear, detailed facts about incidents that happened well before Andrew and Peter "left all".

John 1:35 records that John the Baptist stood *with two of his disciples* and declared that Jesus, whom he had just baptised, was *the Lamb of God.* John was saying that Jesus was the Messiah. We find a few verses later that one of these two disciples of John was none other than Andrew, Peter's brother.

Verse 41 says, *Andrew* ***first*** *findeth his own brother, and said, We have found the Messiah.* It is obvious from this that Andrew and Peter were both waiting for the redemption of Israel, and coming of the Messiah. When they heard this declaration of John, they started to **follow**

Jesus. Andrew and Peter had been disciples of John, but they were not yet disciples of Jesus — they were only followers.

From this account, we can be certain that Peter was not the rough, cursing, godless fisherman of our myths. If he was a disciple of John the Baptist then we can be quite sure he had repented of his sins and been baptized, for this is what John preached and demanded of his followers. Verse 41 tells us that Andrew and Peter were looking for the Messiah, and Acts 10:14 clearly states that Peter had *never eaten anything common or unclean.* He was a good Jew, waiting for the Messiah and following God's prophet, John the Baptist — the only prophet there was to follow before Jesus began his ministry.

Peter, from being a **disciple** of John, had now become a **follower** of Jesus. We now need to look at Luke 4:37 through to 5:11 to find the details of where and how Peter had his "ear pierced". Verse 38 records that Jesus healed Peter's mother-in-law in Peter's own house. Notice that it was not his mother-in-law's house; Jesus was in Peter's own house, so Peter still had his home at this time — he had not yet "left all". *The same day Jesus healed multitudes of people of all manner of diseases, and demons were cast out of many.* Peter was clearly there with Jesus, as a "follower", when Jesus did these healings and preached through the towns of Galilee.

Not quite there

In Luke 5:1-3, we read that Jesus used the boat belonging to Peter and preached to the multitudes from it. Obviously, Peter had still not "left all" at this stage;

he was still a follower. Later he did leave his home, his fishing, his all.

There is nothing wrong with being at this "following" stage. God used Peter's business to an advantage. His boat made an ideal platform. God will also use us in our business, our family situation, or whatever our circumstances may be; but we must realise that this is just "following", and the time of challenge must, and will, come to us all. However, because of fear, which is unbelief, many Christians cannot or will not pay the cost of discipleship, and they remain in the wilderness for the rest of their lives — eating the supernatural spiritual food, having God provide supernaturally for their material needs, but never overcoming the giants and possessing the promised land. So once again God has to wait for the next generation to bring revival to our needy lands.

The miracle

Luke's gospel gives us all the details of Peter's call to discipleship, and we can learn lessons from it ourselves, because the **process** never changes. God will only change the **circumstances** to deceive the faithless. In chapter 5:4, Jesus told Peter, *Launch out and cast your net over the boat for a catch.* Peter had caught nothing all night, but now he found that the nets were breaking. They filled both boats with fish, so much so that they were beginning to sink.

An unusual miracle; it is not easy to understand why Jesus did it. We can understand why he healed people, or fed five thousand hungry men; but what did this miracle accomplish? This was a miracle of **provision**.

Peter was not a collector who kept fish in an aquarium, nor was he an angler who threw them back once he'd caught them. Peter turned fish into money. Fishing to him was not a hobby or pastime; it was his living. He saw fish simply as money.

Before we look at Peter's reaction to this tremendous provision, we must stop and consider what our own reaction would be in the same circumstances; otherwise we will miss a very important lesson.

Let us imagine that we had been following John the Baptist and looking for the Messiah, and that now we have found him and are following him. We are in a supernatural ministry, seeing signs and wonders, when suddenly Jesus does a personal miracle of provision. Maybe this miracle provides many weeks' wages in one moment. What would our reaction be? We might well have seen this as the sign for which we have been waiting. Let me explain. Many modern followers of Jesus would love to go "full time". The only problem stopping them is one of provision. Who will pay the bills? How will they survive without a regular income and pension? They have so many responsibilities and they know that they are *worse than an infidel* if they do not provide for their families. But here is Jesus providing the money **in advance**. Who would not go "full time" if money was paid in their bank account in advance every month?

Strange reaction

Even if we did not see this as a sign of provision to go full time, we would be excited at such a tremendous miracle of blessing. Surely we would have been full of thanks and praise to Jesus. The reaction of Peter was therefore quite amazing, and certainly not predictable.

He reacted in the opposite way to what I would consider to be reasonable. Peter said to Jesus in verse 8, *I cannot follow you any longer. Depart from me.*

Whatever could have caused Peter to make this amazing statement? The answer is in the second half of Peter's sentence: *I am a sinful man.* How could a miracle of provision reveal to Peter his own sinfulness? I do not have an explanation, because God does not use the same circumstances with us all; but I believe I can explain the principle.

The principle

To be a follower of Jesus we need to see **God;** his character needs to be revealed to us — his mercy, grace, forgiveness, truth, provision, eternal life. However, this cannot happen to us without a miracle taking place, because *the god of this world has blinded the eyes of those who don't believe.* The Holy Spirit has to remove this blindfold for the revelation of Christ to be seen. It is then very easy to follow, when the scales fall from our eyes and we see the wonder of God's character.

Discipleship, however, is completely different. Before we can become disciples, another blindfold needs to be removed, and again we cannot remove it ourselves. It has to be an act of God, but this time we have to see **ourselves**. God has to show us **our own character**, the character of Adam which is still in us even after we have received forgiveness. This is unpleasant, in fact it is extremely painful.

Isaiah had the very same experience. He had a vision in chapter 6 of God, high and lifted up in all his glory and majesty. But then Isaiah saw himself, and said, *Woe is me, for I am undone.* There is no other process possible than this. To see God in truth is to see ourselves in truth. I am afraid, however, that many people only see the God of their doctrines. Unfortunately, doctrines can never show us our sinful state. We do not need an explanation of God's character; we need God himself.

Peter saw himself, and he did not like it. He felt that he was unworthy. But this was exactly what Jesus intended, and for the same reason he will do the same to us. Only a person who sees himself as he really is can be a disciple. Peter felt unworthy because he saw his own sinfulness; but Jesus didn't think Peter was unworthy. It seems as if Jesus was completely happy with Peter knowing he was a sinful man. Jesus was saying to him, "*Fear not*, Peter — I have known exactly what you were like all along. I know you will even deny me and say you never knew me. I just want **you** to know it. Now that you do know it, I can really use you. Now I can *make you a fisher of men*".

Useful to God

While Peter was a follower, Jesus was of great use to him. He healed his mother-in-law, he provided a ministry for Peter to be involved in — but as yet Peter was not of any use to Jesus.

But after Jesus revealed to Peter his own sinful state, and Peter acknowledged the truth of this revelation, then **immediately** he became useful to Jesus. He left all and changed from fishing for fish (looking after his own interests) to fishing for men (looking after the interests of the kingdom of God). Here is another principle: God is of great use to followers, but disciples are of great use to God.

The real thing at last

Luke records in chapter 5:11 the same thing that Matthew said in his brief statement: *And when they had brought their ships to land* ***they left all and followed Jesus***. Amazingly, Peter's reaction to the miracle of provision was to forsake all provision. At the very moment when he could have seen in that miracle the answer to all his material needs, he was completely unconcerned about these material needs — instead he was confronted with the needs of his soul. He saw that, provision or no provision, he was not worthy. He could not follow Jesus. But when Jesus encouraged him, he knew he must leave all, and, forsaking the huge catch that could have made him so much money, he instead *left all and followed Jesus.*

True discipleship

This is discipleship. **To follow without leaving all is not discipleship**. How can I be so dogmatic as to say this? I will only refer you to the statements Jesus made concerning the subject. You will have to decide whether you accept them as statements of truth, or as some mystical, spiritual mind set that will satisfy your chosen lifestyle. In Matt.7:24-27, Jesus tells a parable, at the end of the Sermon on the Mount, about building a house on rock or sand. It has been said that Jesus is the rock upon which we build, but this is actually not the case at all. If you look at the parable, Jesus tells us exactly what the rock and the sand mean. Those who build on the rock are those who believe the Sermon on the Mount **and do it**. The ones who build on the sand are those who believe the Sermon on the Mount **and do not do it**. This clearly means that it is the doing, and not the believing, that is the important thing — for how can we prove we believe unless our belief has some visible manifestation? We cannot hide behind our so-called faith if we do not practise what faith demands throughout the whole bible — obedience.

Read carefully the statements of Jesus concerning discipleship. Consider them, for they are far more radical than anything that I have said so far.

The real Christians

Jesus explains in his Sermon on the Mount that **we** are the salt, and that it is not some quality that we sprinkle on society. It is our own personal lives. True Christianity is not what we believe but how we live. Jesus calls it "**the life**", not "**the belief**". There are Christians who believe, and prove it by their lifestyle, and there are those who only believe that they believe, because it is all in their doctrines and thinking.

Luke 14:34-35 — *Salt is good: but if the salt has lost its savour, how shall it be seasoned? It is neither fit for the land, nor for the dunghill; but it is cast out by men.* What power there is in this statement of Jesus — and what an indictment when he says that to lose or not have this life renders us unfit even for the rubbish tip. We become good for nothing.

We have already looked at the principle of slavery in chapter 2, the purchase of men. It is obvious from our example that our good master, God, will not confront us with the challenge of discipleship until we have had time to consider the cost. We need time to consider if we can trust the rest of our life to this master.

Our challenge may come after six years or six months or maybe twenty years; but I am convinced that every follower has at least one call to be a disciple. Israel had only one chance to enter the promised land, but Peter received a second call from Jesus — with exactly the same miracle.

I do not know how it will be for you, because Christianity is a personal relationship with God. You may have ten chances, or you may have only one. What I am saying is that it would be foolish to presume that you will get more than one chance. I know that the principles do not change.

Confrontation

My own experience is that I followed Jesus from the age of six. Twenty-four years later, when I was thirty, I was confronted with the challenge of completely abandoning my own life, having no more say in the remainder of it, and following Jesus wherever he would lead me.

This is a fearful step, because no-one can tell you where Jesus will walk. You may have to follow him to martyrdom, or obscurity, to loneliness or the rejection of men. It is completely out of your hands, and it is this fact that so many followers cannot face. They also want to have a say in their own future.

That is why we need to follow God in a personal relationship, and experience his authority in our lives, before we are asked to make this step. To do it beforehand would be the greatest folly.

From the time I was thirty, I have not looked back, and by the grace of God I will never turn back. My testimony over the last twenty years is that I have found

God to be a good master who only has my welfare at heart. Despite my many failings, I have yet to find an occasion to charge God with anything but faithfulness.

What happens to the followers?

You may be asking, "Are there two classes of Christians then, followers and disciples?" We have seen that there is clearly a progression in the Christian life, and it is impossible to start out as a disciple.

We must, however, banish the thought that God would want two standards of Christians. I can not find any scripture to support this idea. Nevertheless, I am convinced that the majority of people who call themselves Christians are only followers . Many of these have not yet had time to prove God and so have not yet been challenged to leave all; but I believe the majority are those who **have** been challenged, and refused to pay the price. Maybe the call only came to them once, perhaps at a missionary meeting or on a special retreat, or during an illness, or after a bereavement. There are a million circumstances that God may use, but I am convinced that every believer will at some time receive one call to discipleship.

Only the remnant

Am I being presumptuous, bigoted, or self-righteous to claim that the majority have refused the call? I can only say that I have not based my assessment on my own limited and maybe biased judgements, but on my knowledge of the bible and its honest report of God and his dealings with his people.

It is always a remnant, a small minority, who are saved. Noah and his family were saved, and the whole world was drowned. The proportions are frightening. Lot and his family were saved, and a whole area of cities was destroyed.

Perhaps you would argue that the people who were destroyed in these cases were sinners. True, but it is no different with God's people. The whole nation of Israel were delivered from Egypt by signs and wonders, and were clearly "following God"; yet only **two** of them entered the promised land — two out of two million! In the parable of the ten virgins, only half of them went into the marriage feast, and the other half were shut out.

Thousands of people followed Jesus when he walked on the earth, and yet only one hundred and twenty were in the upper room, waiting as Jesus had commanded. Where were the thousands of people he healed and fed in the wilderness? What happened to the crowds who shouted "Hosanna" as Jesus was coming into Jerusalem, when they thought he was going to be made king? I will tell you. They were looking for a Messiah who would make their life easier, and do miracles for them, feed their hungry bodies; but to follow a man to the cross — that was too great a cost.

Part 2
The Cost

No more
It is enough I cry
I cannot bear the awful shame
My eyes no longer look aright
They turn inside
I see myself
Blackness
sin

My body can no longer stand
Knees bend beneath the load
Body lays upon the ground
Lifeless
still

But what is this upon my brow
I feel a drop of liquid fall
And with great effort turn my head
And gaze upon this wondrous sight
Of bleeding hands and wounded feet
And from his side a river flows
Which covers me
And more besides
My heart and soul are sanctified

No more the fear of guilt and shame
My heart is light
My spirit free

Yet still a slave
To serve him more

Maurice Barratt

CHAPTER 4

The Principles

There is a great cost to be paid when a person becomes a disciple, and we need to consider this cost before we can make a decision that will influence our whole lifestyle. I want to look more closely at this cost, for Jesus laid out the conditions very plainly indeed.

Strange instructions

In Matthew 16:16 we read that Peter had a revelation that Jesus was *the Christ, the Son of the living God.* Jesus says that Peter did not come to this conclusion by himself, but that it was a divine revelation. Now that Peter and the other disciples knew this, it would be reasonable to expect that Jesus would commission them to spread this good news, that the Messiah they had waited for had now arrived. They could now with authority and confidence proclaim this revelation to the world.

But in verse 20 Jesus says something quite to the contrary. *Then Jesus charged his disciples that they should tell no man that he was Jesus the Christ.* Why would Jesus give this strange commandment to his disciples? Why would he want this fact hidden? The secret is in verse 21: *From that time forward, Jesus began to show to his disciples that he must go to Jerusalem, and suffer many things, and be killed.*

A change of ministry

If you read the rest of Matthew's gospel from this point, you will find that the ministry of Jesus changes. Apart from one incident where Jesus heals a boy with whom the disciples had difficulties, there are no more healings recorded. Jesus now begins to prepare himself and his disciples to fulfil his purpose on earth, which was to suffer, die an atoning death, and be raised from the dead. This was the real reason Jesus came to earth. The miracles and healings were to only show the character of his Father — love, compassion, mercy and grace. The miracles were not demonstrations of Jesus' power, nor proof that he was the Christ. If they had been demonstrative proofs, then Jesus failed, because the people did not believe him; he was crucified as a blasphemer.

Peter could not understand this change of direction in Jesus' ministry. Like so many Christians today, he was looking for the outward kingdom to be immediately manifested on the earth. Jesus therefore had to rebuke Peter in the strongest language possible. He used exactly the same words to Peter that he used to speak to the devil after the temptations in the wilderness — *Get thee behind me, Satan.* Why such strong language? It was because Jesus was being offered the kingdoms of this world, immediately, and without the cross. This is the modern "kingdom now" doctrine that offers the kingdom without the cross. Peter did not want Jesus to go to the cross because he wanted the kingdom immediately, and without any suffering or hardship. I believe the saying "no cross, no crown" is a true one and is always applicable.

Three simple steps

Jesus, having now firmly established the way he must go, makes it very clear that this is also the way his disciples must go. Verse 24 says, *If any man will come after me, let him deny himself, and take up his cross, and follow me.* Three simple instructions — and yet these are some of the most difficult words that Jesus ever uttered, and we must examine them in detail, for these three steps are the secrets that contain the essence of the entire Christian life.

On first examination, it would seem that Jesus has put these three instructions in the wrong order. Surely, following should be the first step, and then, when we are further along the way, perhaps we could consider whether we should deny ourselves a little. The cross sounds so frightening that to most Christians it is far safer to put it last on the list, and hope that it never comes.

We know that Jesus was a master teacher, so what was his purpose for presenting the lifestyle of a disciple in this order? He can only have meant that unless we have denied self, and taken up our cross, then we are not truly following Jesus. Perhaps we are following our church, or our denomination, our doctrines, our favourite evangelists, or our conscience, but we deceive ourselves if we think that we are following Jesus. Following is only a natural consequence of fulfilling the first two conditions.

I believe that these three statements of Jesus deal with three things we know very well in our lives, the three things which hinder us most in our Christian walk: the world, the flesh and the devil. I believe that denying yourself is the way to deal with the world, taking up the cross is the way to deal with the flesh (our old Adamic nature), and following Jesus, the natural consequence, is the way to deal with the devil. Once we have dealt with the world and the flesh, we will naturally have power over the devil — but only then.

Destroying the work of the devil

In 1 John 3:8 we are told that *Jesus was manifested to destroy the works of the devil.* What is the work of the devil? The opposite of the work of God. What is God's work? It is **to make men holy**. The devil's work is the opposite — to cause men to rebel against God and become like himself, **unholy**. To destroy the work of the devil, then, is simply to undo or reverse this process and bring men back into fellowship and obedience to God, so that their characters become like God's. This is the whole purpose of the church, to make men holy.

If we have not left this world, and if our old nature has not been dealt with, that is, crucified, how can we possibly become holy? Destroying the devil's work is the third and final stage. For this, we need the **character** of Christ, not just his **power**, for the devil is not afraid of power unless it is accompanied by holiness. He can substitute all the power and all the gifts, but he can never be holy or show the character of Christ.

Let us now look closely at each of these three conditions which Jesus presents to us.

CHAPTER 5

Deny Yourself

Self-denial has nothing to do with sin. For those who are Christians, the atoning blood of Jesus has paid the legal requirements for all our sins and, as English law confirms, a crime can only be paid for once. Jesus paid the price for our crime in full, and we now have the righteousness of Christ, not self-righteousness. There is nothing that can make us any more or less righteous than we are under the blood of Christ, and our righteousness in Christ doesn't change because of our circumstances or weaknesses. It is a fixed state. Jesus' death is a perfect atonement.

However, I am sure that any honest Christian will admit that they continue to sin even after they have accepted this atonement, for anything less than perfection is sin. The difference is that now we are no longer accountable for our sins. As Paul says in Romans 8:1, *There is therefore now no condemnation to them which are in Christ Jesus, who walk not after the flesh, but after the Spirit.* And in Colossians 1 verses 21 and 22, Paul says, *And you ... hath he now reconciled in the body of his flesh through death, to present you holy and unblameable and unreproveable in his sight.* As Martin

Luther rightly stated, we are always sinners and yet always justified.

Let me speak from my own experience, and trust that yours is the same. The last thing I want to do is to sin, and yet I can echo Paul's words and say that I sin despite my desires. I crave to be like my Saviour, and perfect in every way, but in practice I sin daily because of my Adamic nature. Therefore, to deny myself sin would not be self-denial. It would be a pleasure!

Denying legitimate things

If this is true, then self-denial can only mean one thing. It means denying myself **things that I like doing**, pleasures that are legitimate, things that are not sinful in themselves. This is why Jesus and the apostles talked so much about the world, and the dangers of it.

We need to be clear here that when the Bible talks about "the world" it does not mean the earth, God's creation. *The earth is the Lord's and all that is in it,* but the god of this present age is *the god of this world,* Satan. Unlike the earth, which is a physical creation, the world does not exist in any physical form. It is a spiritual system, a way of thinking. It includes culture, politics, commerce and religion.

In 2 Corinthians 4:4 Paul says that *the god of this world has blinded people's eyes.* This can only be Satan. Our present world, since Adam's first sin, has never belonged to anyone else except Satan, and will never belong to anyone except Satan. This state of affairs will never change until the prophecy in Revelation 11:15 is fulfilled, when *the kingdoms of this world will become the kingdoms of our Lord and of his Christ.*

When we consider the following Scriptures regarding the world, it should be obvious that, as Christians, we should deny ourselves and be separate from the world.

Matthew 16:26 — *For what is a man profited if he shall gain the whole world, and lose his own soul?* (We take this scripture out of context when we use it as in a gospel message to sinners. It is spoken to disciples of Jesus.)

Mark 4:19 — *The cares of this world and the deceitfulness of riches, and the lusts of other things entering in, choke the word, and it becomes unfruitful.* This is another scripture that applies to people who have received God's word and have already borne fruit.

James 4:4 — *Do you not know that the love of the world makes you the enemy of God, and that it is spiritual adultery?* Again, this word is spoken to Christians.

1 John 2:15-16 — *Love not the world, neither the things that are in the world. If any man love the world, the love of the Father is not in him. For all that is in the world, the lust of the flesh, the lust of the eyes and the pride of life, is not of the Father, but of the world.* Once again, a scripture spoken to the church.

Leaving the world

It is easy for Christians to **talk** about being not of this world, but how do we relate to this fact in our everyday life, at work, or in our family situations? I am excluding our church life, for I believe that generally it is a false situation. Our Christianity is how we act and live in our life **outside** the church, not how we behave in the church. I am as much a Christian as when I lose my temper with my wife, when I tell my boss I am not well so that I can decorate my house, or when I have an immoral thought at church when everyone else seems to be praising and worshipping God.

Christianity is what I really am, and how God sees me. It is not what I **believe** I am, or what I **profess** that I am. Christianity is to do with the heart; otherwise it is a false religion, and vanity.

Most evangelical Christians would accept that to leave the world physically and go into a monastery is not what Jesus intended for the majority of his followers. He said that we have to be **in** the world but not **of** it. However, we must not be too critical of people who do go into a monastery to escape the world. Unless we can live the monastic lifestyle in the world, then we should only admire these people who have the courage to act out their convictions.

The world leaving us

Jesus clearly said that the world is of the devil and we are not to love it. To do so is spiritual adultery and very serious indeed. To put it in a nutshell we can say this: If we want to be disciples, either we have to leave the world, **or the world has to leave us.**

The writings of John and Charles Wesley are full of this message. Were they misguided and out of date? History has surely proved the very opposite; in fact some scholars have traced the roots of the whole modern Pentecostal Charismatic movement to this very period of church history, and to these two men.

What our societies need today is not more miracle workers, or more superstar evangelists (who will weep for souls for a price), but holy men of God — men who like Paul count all things as dung to win Christ. There never has been, and never will be, any other way to true revival.

Let me quote from a couple of Wesley's hymns which seem to have been buried under the profusion of worship and praise songs of late.

Let nothing now my heart divide
Since with thee I am crucified
And live to God in thee
Dead to the world and all its toys
Its idle pomp and fading joys
Jesus my glory be

Refining fire go through my heart
Illuminate my soul
Scatter thy life through every part
And sanctify the whole

It is obvious to everybody that a person who goes to live in a monastery, or some other place of seclusion, has left the world; but it is much more difficult to discern whether the world has left them. It is so easy to deceive ourselves. How can we know, or prove to ourselves, that the world has left us? Jesus said just before he was crucified, *The prince of this world comes, but he has no part in me.* What did he mean? Simply this: that there was no part of Jesus that desired anything that the devil could offer. The bible tells us in James 1:13-14 that *God tempts no man ... we are drawn away by our own desires.* So if our desires are pure, we can not be tempted.

Here is a test for us to apply. Anything at all that we can not live without must have a hold over us, and if it has a hold over us, then this can only mean that we are not completely free.

If you feel you can not live without money, a car, your husband or wife, your health, music or sports, then you are not free. Let us remind ourselves again that denying self is to do with denying **legitimate** things. No-one would suggest that a family, music or sports are sinful things. But let us not forget that *whosoever he be of you that forsaketh not all that he hath, he cannot be my disciple.*

Throughout church history Christians have found this concept so difficult to understand, and invariably swing from one extreme to another. The two following examples will illustrate my point.

Television

When television first became available to the public, many ministers called it the "hellivision". Yet these same ministers now have a television in their own homes. Were they right in the first instance, and have they now backslidden, or are they right now and were misled and over-reacting before? We have to be careful not to fall on one side or the other; both extremes are wrong. Television is a neutral medium, but its message is not neutral. The sin is that of the programme makers, not the medium itself. It could be used to preach the gospel. Television has had a fearful effect on our societies and its influence has affected the church, and not for good.

I think you have to be a very strong Christian to have a Television and not be influenced by it, that is, conditioned to the world's way of thinking. The millions of pounds spent on advertising prove that repetition of the same message, the same values, the same ethos, will influence us with or without our consent. To be in the world and not of it is not easy. To have a television and not be influenced by it is very difficult indeed.

Money

Money is another good example of this principle, although the same will be true for any of this world's powers.

Finance has a power of its own. The bible calls it *filthy lucre* and *unrighteous mammon.* These are derogatory terms. A disciple is one who has divested money of its power so that it becomes neutral and can be used as such for the kingdom of God. The money then has no power over this person. He is not dependent on it for his contentment, security, or life. He is as happy without it as he is with it. His security comes from God alone. In the Sermon on the Mount Jesus said, *Take no thought for food, clothing, or even life itself.* Notice he said *Take no* ***thought***. He means "do not worry". Do not let these things have any power over you.

Jesus did have a treasurer amongst his disciples, Judas who "had the bag", but it seems to me that the money was not to provide food and clothing for himself, or his disciples (and it is easy to forget that twelve hungry men take some feeding). I believe he relied on God for these things, and we know that God provided wealthy women to supply their needs in this area.

Money for taxes? There was none. They needed a miracle. Jesus had the purse **for other people's needs**. The bag was to feed the poor. What did covetous Judas say at the supposed waste of Mary's costly ointment? He did not say "this money could have clothed and fed us for a few weeks". He said, *Why was not this sold and given to the* *poor?* Even greedy Judas knew why they had money, and how it had to be used.

Jesus was so unconcerned about money that he allowed Judas, whom he knew from the beginning to be a thief, to be the treasurer. In Matthew 10, in his instructions to the disciples as he sent them out to preach and minister, he commanded that they should take no money with them. This sounds radical, and of course it is, but because the world has such a vice-like grip that we need a radical approach to break free of its hold over us.

No one leaves Egypt without a struggle

Most bible scholars agree that in scripture, Egypt typifies the world. Egypt needed ten devastating plagues before Pharaoh finally allowed God's people to go; and it is no different today in our own lives in this world's system. The world does not leave us easily. If your securities as a Christian are the same as those of the world, then you would have a very hard time convincing me that your Christianity is anything more than an idea in your mind. To say that you serve the living God, who created all things, and that he is like a father to you; to say that you are an alien, and your true home is now in heaven, is easy. But it becomes a mockery and an insult to the teaching of Jesus and the apostles if you don't live a different lifestyle.

The truth is that most Christians do not really believe in heaven. The last thing they want is to be released from this life. They enjoy it too much, and their treasures are securely on this earth, and not in heaven at all. I could mention politics, fashion, insurance, entertainment, sport and many more areas where Christians have just followed the thinking and dictates of the world, not realising that by doing so they are constantly and consistently "laying up treasures on earth", the very thing Jesus told us not to do.

History has shown that the church has always assimilated the mind-set of the world. In times of monarchy the churches support the monarchy, and under democratic governments, churches support democracy and run their own structures democratically as though this was God's chosen method for government. A little leaven permeates the whole lump and corruption very quickly sets in. The salt quickly loses its savour.

True Christianity must be apolitical, and Christians should be a threat to **all** political systems. Surely the kingdom of God is a real alternative to any system that the god of this world has to offer.

Persecution or conformity

History records that the early church was considered by the Romans as a subversive threat to their civil and political systems, and they persecuted them as such. The persecution only ceased when Constantine accepted Christianity and made it the official religion of the Roman Empire; and we were then plunged into a thousand years of stagnation and sordid church history. This is appropriately referred to as the Dark Ages.

The same thing would happen today if the church were to gain control of the world systems, as so many of our prophets are suggesting it should and will — I mean the push towards the so-called Christianising of the arts, culture, politics, and so on, as if these worldly powers can in some mysterious way be "redeemed".

The culmination of this process would see the church invested with political power and the politicians invested with religious powers — a complete perversion of what Jesus clearly taught. I can only look at the terrible mistakes of church history and say, God forbid that it should ever happen again.

We must live in the world, but we must also think and act differently from the world, liberated from all powers that belong to the world's system. They must be stripped of their influence over us so that, rather than them being a threat to us, we become a threat to them.

Normal Christianity

As we look more closely at the teaching of Jesus we will be left in no doubt that this is what he is expecting from his disciples. This is no more than the normal Christian life. Why is this so daunting a proposition to many people? Jesus often said things like, *My yoke is easy and my burden light ... I have not come to condemn you, but to give you a more abundant life.* Why do people fall on one side of the fence or the other? They either dismiss the challenge of the cross as unattainable and too negative for a modern society, or they adhere to the "dead letter" of the law and become sanctimonious hypocrites — the most miserable of religious people.

I have come to the conclusion that both categories of people are misguided simply because they do not understand the process. They miss the great joy that is derived when holiness is unassuming and not a matter of willpower. In the following chapters I hope I can convince you that this process is very simple and extremely realistic, and one that need not be feared.

CHAPTER 6

Take up Your Cross

The congregation were singing "Speak my Lord, speak to me, speak and I'll be quick to answer Thee" — then God did speak. His voice ripped through the heavens and thundered into the church where I sat with this congregation of God's people. My legs shook like jelly, so powerful was the voice of the Lord. He said, "Go up the mountain, separate and sanctify yourself." God had spoken, I knew I had to obey. My body automatically stood up and walked out of the church and travelled towards the mountain.

As my body walked, my spirit left it for a minute to look back at the place I had just left. I expected to see the rest of the congregation walking towards the mountain also. I was amazed, for no-one else had heard God's voice, or if they had they had not responded. So loud it had been, and yet no-one had heard it.

I reached the bottom of the mountain and looked up. "Lord," I asked, "Is this necessary, it seems such a waste? If I go up the mountain I'll only have to come down again." God had spoken and I was too afraid to disobey, so I set off up the side of the mountain.

At first it was mossy, but it soon changed to hard rock that ripped my shoes to ribbons and rendered them useless. Night fell, and I looked for a place where I might sleep, but there was no bed or soft pillow for me to lie upon. Again my spirit left my body and I looked back from my elevated position to see the place I had left. I could see the people leaving the church and going home to the comforts of their houses, warm beds and soft pillows, and I said, "Lord, is this necessary?" But God had spoken, and I had to obey.

When I awoke in the morning I was very hungry. I travelled further up the mountain and still found no food. It was like being on an enforced fast. My spirit left my body again to look back and I saw the people eating and drinking their sumptuous fare, marrying and giving in marriage, and I realised what I had left behind. I asked again, "Lord, is this really necessary?" But God had spoken, and I had to obey.

At last I reached the summit, but I hadn't been prepared for what I saw there. This was the supreme test of my obedience. My body fought strongly against it, "Lord, is this necessary?" Before me I could see a sacrificial altar of cold stone, and by the side of it the knife which would kill the sacrifice. I wanted very much to give up at this stage but I had come this far and it seemed even worse than death to disobey the voice of the Lord.

The scripture from Romans 12:1 came to my mind, ***Present your bodies a living sacrifice which is only***

> ***your reasonable service.*** *So I lay down on the slab and plunged the knife into my body. As I did this another scripture from Matthew 16:25 came to my mind,* ***He that would save his life shall lose it, but he that would lose his life for my sake shall find it.*** *Then I saw my spirit leave my body again, and this time it did not return, for my flesh was dead. Now I was totally free, for it had been the flesh that had experienced all the suffering and discomfort, hunger and death, not my spirit. At last I had been freed so I could go back down the mountain to do God's will without any hindrances at all.*
>
> **Joanna Barratt**

Let us now look at the second condition that Jesus presents to a person who is called to be a disciple: *Take up your cross.* The first condition, *deny yourself,* is about the world and how we are to live in it without being part of it; it is to do with our outward lifestyle. But this second condition is completely different. It is to do with our inward, or secret life.

The wrong cross

It always amazes me how many different circumstances Christians will call their cross. Here are a few commonly heard examples; I'm sure you have come across all these:

A sickness that persists even after medication and prayer. In desperation a person will say, "I will just have to bear it. It must be my cross."

A person married to an unbeliever. Their minister and friends pray for their partner, but nothing seems to change. They fast and pray but don't know what else to do, so they say, "It must be my cross. I suppose every Christian has one".

Work situations often seem to bring out our "crosses". "My boss has it in for me because I'm a Christian. He waits for an opportunity to find fault with my work. I've prayed that God would find me a new job; I've prayed that my boss would leave; but we're both still here. It must be my cross to keep me humble".

Common to man

We can straight away dispense with these so-called crosses. These examples are all situations relating to outward circumstances that we would like to change. I am not saying that these circumstances are good, or that they don't need changing; what I want to prove is that they have nothing at all to do with our cross. I will give two reasons to support my statement. The first is this: if these outward circumstances are the cross, then everyone in the world must have a cross to bear at some time in their life, because as Paul says in 1 Corinthians 10:13, such circumstances are *common to man.*

The circumstances that happen to non-Christians also happen to Christians. Contrary to the belief of many Christians, God does not offer them a trouble-free or charmed life. The bible does not say that we will be preserved from the same conditions, problems and circumstances that the world faces.

An experiment

Try this little experiment if you have any doubts at all. Write down the names of ten Christians. Include your pastor and your favourite evangelist. Then write down the names of ten people that you know are not Christians. Include your boss from work and perhaps some celebrity.

Now, compare honestly their experiences of life and you will find that there is no difference. You will find that Christians have had car crashes, died before old age, lost children at an early age, and had heart attacks — all the things that are common to all people. Conversely, some non-Christians seem to live charmed lives! Health, wealth and contentment seem to follow them whatever they do. Read Ecclesiastes for Solomon's assessment of this subject. This should be evidence enough that the cross we are asked to take up is not our outward circumstances.

Take up your cross

The second reason why difficult or even tragic circumstances are not the cross is this: the circumstances that I have illustrated are to do with situations that we would wish to change, and for this very reason it excludes them from what Jesus is saying. I will quote exactly what Jesus said to emphasise this point. *Let him **take up** his cross.* The cross Jesus is referring to is a cross that **we take up**, not one that is put upon us; and circumstances are always by definition "put upon us". Ask yourself: would you choose to have a sickness, an unhappy marriage, or an unpleasant work environment? Certainly not! Therefore we can put aside the idea that difficult circumstances are anything to do with the cross.

Thus far we have only considered the negative aspects — what the cross is **not** — so we must now carefully decide what it is that we have to positively "take up".

What would it have meant to Peter and the other disciples when they heard these words? To them it would have been obvious, for they were under Roman occupation, and thousands of lawbreakers were crucified on Roman crosses. The humiliation for many of these criminals was that they had to carry the very cross on which they were to be hung. The disciples knew that there was only one reason anyone would take up a cross — to be crucified.

Death to self

Dietrich Bonhoeffer, in his book "The Cost of Discipleship", says that "when Christ calls a man, he bids him come and die". This is not an alarmist or extreme claim. There is no other possible alternative. Jesus was not saying that we should be physically crucified, for in Luke's gospel he says, *take up your cross* ***daily***; nevertheless there can be no other interpretation to Jesus' words than death. So what then has to die, if it is not our mortal life? Paul can help us to understand, for he talks about being crucified in his letters to the churches.

Romans 6:6 states, *Our old man is crucified with Jesus.* Paul in context is talking about baptism, but it clearly gives us a connection with the "old man". This is the same as the flesh, both being terms for the sinful rebellious nature that we all inherit at birth from Adam.

In Galatians 5:24, just after Paul has contrasted the works of the flesh (old nature) with the fruit of the spirit (the new nature of Christ), he says, *And they that are Christ's have crucified the flesh with the affections and lusts.*

These two Scriptures clearly show us what must be crucified in a Christian. It is not our outward life but our inward character. This is why taking up the cross is completely different to denying ourselves. Denying ourselves deals with our outward behaviour and lifestyle; taking up the cross deals with our inward character, the flesh. This is the whole purpose of our Christian life, to change from Adam's character to the character of our new master, Christ. Paul says in Ephesians 4:11, *God gave apostles, prophets, evangelists, pastors and teachers for the perfecting of the saints ... till we all come unto a perfect man, unto the measure of the stature of the fullness of Christ.*

We must never pretend that death in any form is palatable. Whether in our outward flesh or our inward character, the natural fear of death is common to man. Knowing and facing this fact can actually give us comfort, for our leader and guide *endured the cross for the joy that was set before him.* It does not say he **enjoyed** the cross, it says that he looked beyond it to the joy that awaited him — the resurrection that makes the cross worthwhile.

Crucified with Christ

If Christians could only see beyond the death of self to a new life with the nature of Christ, they would have such a different outlook on their Christianity. What makes death to self such a glorious victory is the resurrection life of Jesus Christ manifested in our mortal body.

An understanding of this makes Paul's declaration in Galatians 2:20 take on a fresh purpose: *I am crucified with Christ: nevertheless I live; yet not I, but Christ lives in me: and the life that I now live in the flesh I live by the faith of the Son of God.*

It is only when self dies that Christ can live his life in me. No one in the flesh can live the Christian life. Only a hypocrite can successfully do it. Christ alone can live the life in us, because he **is** the life, and he will live his life in our bodies if we will die to self. This is true freedom. Paul said that he lived by the faith **of** the Son of God. It was not faith **in** the Son of God. Paul did not even live by his own faith! A dead man cannot have faith. He lived by the faith of Jesus in him. This wonderful fact, that it is Christ's faith, not ours, does away once and for all with our strivings and "mind-over-matter" type of faith, which genders only pride or frustration.

Life for life

Denying self has to do with the world and our outward, visible life in it. But the cross is to do with the flesh, our inward nature which is really **our secret life**, nothing to do with our outward morals. This is to do with the **heart**, the very seat of our ambitions, secret motives, and desires; things which are hidden from our wife or husband, pastor or closest friend, and often even hidden from ourselves.

In the bible "the mind" means our conscious thoughts, but "the heart" means something deeper — our **subconscious** thinking. It is our secret desires, motives, and lusts. We may know **what** we think, but we deceive ourselves if we imagine that we understand **why** we think. The bible tells us to *renew our minds* because we are capable of this conscious process, but it does not tell us to renew our hearts. David asked God to try his heart and search it to see if there was any wicked way in it. Jeremiah 17:9 states that *the heart is deceitful above all things, and desperately wicked: who can know it?* It is so deceitful that it will deceive you into believing that it is pure!

My whole purpose in explaining this is to emphasise that the cross is to do with our **secret life**, and I will refer to it as such for the rest of this chapter.

Let me present three more thoughts about self-crucifixion. The first is that running away from the world and its temptations can never deal with the flesh. We can certainly avoid many temptations that would entice us to sin, by physically removing or avoiding them, but this will never deal with our secret life.

Monasteries can't kill our flesh

A monastery is a prime example of people's genuine desire to protect themselves from the temptations of the flesh; but as such it can only fail, because self is the inner life which a person takes with them into the monastery; no-one can escape from their own self. For example, we could escape outward immorality by living in a monastery, and yet lie on a hard stone bed with little food in our bodies and fantasise immorally and have a burning lust in our heart. I used to be very critical of people who left the world and entered a monastery. I accused them of escapism; but I have since realised that unless I can live that monastic lifestyle whilst still in the world, I have no right to criticise those people who have had the courage of their convictions.

As long as we are alive to self we will have this problem, and accordingly Jesus gives us the only remedy — dying by crucifixion. There is no other solution.

My second thought is that anything with **self-** as a prefix should sound warning bells in our mind. Words such as self-improvement, self-esteem, self-worth, satisfaction (which is only a way of saying self-satisfied), are all ways of keeping self alive and healthy. Jesus said the very opposite: *deny self.* Self is bad; it has to be destroyed. Self is to do with pride and the ego, everything that vaunts itself against God. But how can self deny self? How can we destroy the self that we love? Although it seems impossible, somehow self has to go, for this simple reason: *God will not share his glory with flesh.* Two characters cannot run one body at the same time.

There is a strange doctrine that has become prevalent of late, and many Christians have accepted it without thought. Their line of thinking is similar to this: Jesus said *love your neighbour as yourself,* so you cannot love your neighbour until you learn to love yourself. You need to have a better self-image and start to really love yourself as God loves you.

Twisted logic

This may seem logical at face value, but I believe it is a twisted logic and very dangerous. Let me explain why. The bible says that self-love is the opposite of what God requires, for you can not love God and self at the same time. When people say that they "hate themselves", they are actually deceived. They interpret their feelings as self-hatred, but in fact it is self-pity or inverted pride, because if they really hated themselves they would be happy to have a poor self-image! So these conditions of the heart are the very opposite of what they appear. Self-pity is only a form of self-love, for whenever the attention is on us instead of God we are on dangerous ground. Jesus said we are to **deny** self, not **love** self. Paul says in Ephesians 5:29, *For no man has* *ever hated his own flesh; but nourishes and cherishes it.* Jesus asks us to deny self because he knows that we all instinctively love ourselves and pander to our own desires. He was saying that we should also treat our neighbour in the same instinctive way. Jesus showed in the parable of the Good Samaritan that our neighbour also includes our enemies.

Self-crucifixion is impossible

No honest person could possibly relish the thought of their secret life being exposed and mortified. So my third thought should give us a ray of hope. **It is impossible to crucify yourself**. Crucifixion is not a possible way of suicide. A victim could be willing, but he could not do the deed himself. He would need two hands to knock even the first nail into himself. My point is that what applies to physical crucifixion is also true of the inward crucifixion of the flesh: we cannot do it ourselves.

It is of paramount importance that we grasp this fact. We can progress no further in our walk with God if we do not. People who try to deal with their secret life themselves will find that this can only end in one of two possible results, and neither of them have any effect on the old nature. Either they will assume that they are becoming holy, and act in a more outwardly moral manner (which is only hypocrisy), or else they will be honest with themselves, still see themselves as they are, and feel condemned, doomed to be a second-class Christian, without hope of improvement.

How can the fact that we cannot crucify ourselves be a ray of hope? Let me explain. If we cannot crucify ourselves, then it will have to happen despite us — someone else will have to crucify us; that is, God. It is his work, not ours. The emphasis then changes, because our part is that we have to be willing for it to happen. This is hope indeed, because true holiness (as with all of the beatitudes) must be an unassuming, hidden righteousness which is even hidden from ourselves. Anything we do ourselves is always something we are going to be conscious of, a "work" which we can boast about (to ourselves if not to anyone else). But if the work is not done by us, and we are not conscious of it, our holiness becomes "unassuming".

Dealing with the secret life

I am convinced that God will do this work for us if we are indeed willing, simply because it is the only answer to our problem of how to become holy. It is only more of Jesus in us that makes us like him. Nothing else can do it. All else produces only deceit and hypocrisy.

However, there is one problem. God will not do this work for us just because we ask him. He needs more than our words. Talk in itself is not enough. We may not really mean it. We have to do something to prove our motive and desire, and that is to be obedient to the things that Jesus tells us to do, things that are not too difficult for us, things that we **can** do. We have to do these things, to prove to God that we mean what we say, before he will change the things which we **cannot** do — the things we have been trying to do but are giving us problems.

The answer to the problem of our secret life is another secret life — what I call **the secret life of a disciple**. In

Matthew 6, Jesus tells us three things that we must do in secret. The reason we are to do these things is in order to prove our motives to God, and to ourselves; to prove to God that we are doing it for his praise alone, not the praise of men. This is a great key to the Christian life, and the things Jesus asks us to do are all very possible, even to a new convert.

Let us remember that the cross is something that we take up, not something which is put upon us. We have to actively take up this secret life. Luke's gospel says we must take it up daily. Holiness is not an act or a belief; it is a process, and that implies time. There is no quick way to be holy. Experience and suffering are all part of the process. Paul says in 2 Timothy 3:12, *All those who would live godly in Christ Jesus will suffer persecution*; and in Hebrews 2:10, *The captain of our salvation was perfected through sufferings.* How blind must a Christian be to think that blessings alone could change our character for the better! Unfortunately, blessings are more likely to swell our heads than our hearts. Success rarely humbles a man or makes him holy.

Walking in the Spirit

I am convinced that only a secret life with God, the secret life of the disciple, doing the things that Jesus commands, can counteract the secret life of Adam which we have inherited, and which we all have to battle with daily.

Let me close this section with the words of Paul in Galatians 5:16. *This I say then, walk in the Spirit, and you shall not fulfil the lust of the flesh.* He does not say that Christians do not have lusts of the flesh. Rather he infers that they do exist, but that if we walk in the Spirit we will not fulfil them. This is entirely different from saying that these lusts, or the old nature, don't exist. Paul tells us we can have victory over them only by continually fulfilling a condition; we must **walk in the Spirit** — that is, in the new nature, the character of Christ. And the only way we can possibly do this is if we allow God to crucify our flesh.

CHAPTER 7

Follow Me

"Follow me" is the third and final instruction that Jesus gave to those who wished to be his disciples. We have already noted that we would expect "following" to be the first condition, and at the start of our Christian walk, not the final stage in the progression. But we must understand that true "following" is only the consequence of obeying the first two instructions.

A natural consequence

This is the only way to be a real follower. A man who thinks he can follow Jesus without denying himself and taking up his cross is being deceived. A good example is the rich young ruler, who believed he was doing God's will until Jesus exposed him. He went away sorrowful because he was unable, or unwilling, to pay the price of discipleship.

In my comparison of these three instructions with "the world, the flesh and the devil", following Jesus is to do with dealing with the devil. When we consider that following Jesus means going where he went, doing what he did, and when we remember that his purpose was **to destroy the works**

of the devil, we can understand that when we truly reach this stage of following Jesus, we too will destroy the works of the devil — but only if we meet the first two conditions.

The wrong order

The destruction of the devil's work may also appear to be in the wrong place in the sequence. So many Christians think that if they have been saved and filled with the Holy Ghost, then they can immediately start to "smash the devil", before they even think about denying themselves or taking up their cross. Indeed, they may have the **potential** to destroy the devil's works, but that does not qualify them to hold that position before they have become mature.

My little five-year-old boy may have the **potential** to be a Prime Minister, but that certainly does not qualify him for holding the position today! It is maturity that he lacks, and exactly the same problem exists when Christians think that they are mature just because they have been born again. Maturity can never come quickly, because maturity only comes from experience, and experience takes time.

Gifts without fruit

In Corinthians 12:7 Paul says that the nine gifts of the Holy Spirit are *manifestations of the Spirit.* This means that they are visible and observable. Gifts of healing do not happen in our subconscious; they effect physical changes in our body. Paul says the nine gifts all come from the one Spirit. They display the power of God.

There is, however, another list in Galatians 5:22-23: the *fruit of the Spirit.* Again there are nine characteristics, but I believe that these are not to do with power or visible manifestations of God. These attributes or qualities are the **character** of God.

Can a person have the power of God without the character of God? To put it another way, can a person have the gifts without the fruit? We must not be afraid to ask this question, for it is an important one. I am one hundred per cent certain that the answer to both these questions is yes, and in fact it is very often the case with supernatural manifestations. Jesus himself provides one proof of this, for in Matthew 7:22 he said that in the day of reckoning, ***many*** *will say, Lord, Lord, have we not prophesied in your name? and in your name cast out devils? and in your name done many wonderful works*?

They were asking a question, but also protesting their right to enter into the kingdom. What was the answer that Jesus gave to them? Did he refute their claim and say that their miracles were not in his name? No, he accepted that their facts were true, but nevertheless his answer was that *he never knew them.* They were never his children. They were like the Pharisees, who Jesus said were *of their father the devil.* Yet they worked miracles. It is possible to be a child of the devil and do miracles in Jesus' name.

All-powerful God

Let me ask another question which may help our understanding of this.

Did the devil create himself? The answer must be no, because only God can create. If we accept this as a fact, then it is clear that the devil has no power of his own. There is no power in the universe except God's. We can use it or abuse it, but God has all power, which means there is no power left for anyone else. In 1 Corinthians 13, where Paul is contrasting the gifts with the fruit, he says in verse 2, *If I exercise the gifts and have no love* (love is one word that describes all the fruit) *then I AM NOTHING.* God cannot recognise us if there is nothing of his character in us. The gifts prove that we have God's power; but they don't prove whether we are God's children. The devil himself can only use God's power, for there is no other power, and God has given the devil limited power.

Jesus, talking about false prophets and how to recognise them, says in Matthew 7:20, *You shall know them by their fruits* (not by their gifts). He calls those who have gifts and no fruit *wolves in sheep's clothing.* It is hard to understand why the church is so negligent in applying this test, which Jesus gave for our protection.

Dealing with the devil

Our enemy, Satan, is not a fool, nor is he impressed with the name of Jesus, unless the **character** of Jesus is in the person speaking that name. After all, Satan uses the name of Jesus very frequently, as blasphemy. However, he **is** afraid of people who are not part of his system (the world), and of those who have crucified the flesh; that is, holy people. This is why, despite all our Charismatic, Pentecostal power, and all our shouting at the devil and telling him he is defeated, we have not in our western societies brought even one village to repentance in ninety years of testimony. We should carefully consider how our forefathers brought whole communities to repentance without these gifts.

Do these words imply that I am against the gifts of the Spirit? On the contrary, I believe in them all, and I believe that we need them in our present age. I believe in prophecy and visions, angel visitation and gifts of healing, but I know that the **gifts** of the Spirit can never produce **fruit**. They can only produce power. Abiding in the vine is the only thing that will produce fruit.

Our country does not need more followers of Jesus; it needs more disciples of Jesus. It does not need more preachers; it needs more men of God, more **holy** preachers — not men who weep for souls because they are being paid to do so, nor those who will heal the sick because it brings the crowds, fame and finance, but men who will do these things because they have the character of Christ; men who are like Jesus, filled with compassion. There is a world of difference between these two, and even if the church can not recognise it, our enemy Satan can, and that very easily.

Conditions for revival

2 Chronicles 7:14 tells us that four conditions are required for revival, and not one of them is to do with spiritual warfare or battling with the devil. They are to do with God, the judge of all the earth. *If my people will humble themselves, pray, seek my face, and turn from their wicked ways ... I will heal their land.* Revival is God's prerogative and not our right, and that is why we have to meet the conditions and not just say the correct words to God or Satan. Read in the Acts of the Apostles 19:13-16 how the sons of Sceva tried, by saying the right

words, to cast out a devil, with disastrous results. The devil said to them, "**I don't know you**. I know Jesus, I know Paul, but who are you?" Saying the right words, or even doing the right works, is not enough; it's whose character you have within you.

Jesus said in the Sermon on the Mount that many people would stand before him on the judgement day and remind him of the supernatural works they had done in his name. Jesus accepted that they had done these works, but his answer to them was "I don't know you". There was none of his character within them.

I find it very interesting that the devil said exactly the same words as Jesus, "I don't know you". They were both looking for one quality only — the character of Christ.

CHAPTER 8

Moses

The three conditions which Jesus gives us for discipleship are fundamental, and surprisingly, they do not originate in the New Testament. Principles for godly living and the processes for holiness do not change throughout the whole bible. In the following examples from the Old and New Testaments we will see that before God can trust and use a man for his purposes, there always has to be a progression through the three stages — self-denial (dealing with the world), taking up the cross (dealing with the flesh) and following Jesus (dealing with the devil).

Leaving Egypt

Moses was reared in Egypt, a great cultural empire, and educated as Pharaoh's son. If Egypt typifies the world, as most bible scholars agree, Moses was becoming great and successful in the world. He was brought up in all the eloquence and pride of this great nation.

Under provocation, Moses did what was natural for his Adamic nature to do. He saw one of his fellow Hebrews being mistreated, murdered the Egyptian oppressor, and freed a man under bondage. This was not a permanent solution, of course, for doubtless another taskmaster just as cruel would replace the dead man. It was only a temporary alleviation; but God had a greater purpose — he used these circumstances, for Moses had to flee for his life.

Destiny

I am sure that anyone whom God intends to use has a sense of destiny, and I believe that Moses felt deep down that someday he would deliver God's people. However, he did not realise that you cannot deliver people from the world when you are still in it yourself. Thomas à Kempis in his book "The Imitation of Christ" said, "You can not take anyone further than you are willing to go yourself". So Moses had to leave the world.

Having left Egypt, Moses now began the second stage of his training and spiritual progress. He went into the wilderness for forty years, and looked after sheep, an occupation that was an abomination to an Egyptian. It was not enough for him to leave Egypt (the world); he now had to have his inner life crushed, the pride of Egypt in his soul. All of its culture and thinking had to be destroyed in his life.

Moses' call

When God called him, Moses claimed that he was not eloquent — *a man of stammering lips*. Was this a speech impediment from birth? The bible does not say so. Was it a lack of faith, or fear of Pharaoh? I do not believe so. I believe Moses had now come to a true assessment of himself. He had been trained in the protocol of Egypt, and was well qualified to do the job; after all, he had been brought up in Pharaoh's palace.

After forty years in the wilderness, Moses now had a true assessment of himself. He had no confidence in self. This was a healthy situation, for now he could only have confidence in God. John Wesley's definition of humility was "having a true assessment of yourself". This makes you weak in self, but strong in God.

The wilderness had accomplished this process in Moses. Talking to sheep for forty years had robbed him of his confidence in the flesh, all the eloquence and pride that was natural to Egypt's culture. After this, God's assessment was that Moses was *the meekest man on earth.* I think it is worth forty years of trials to have an accolade like that from God.

God was now ready to use Moses, because Moses was now ready to be used by God. Now he was ready for the third stage, which is a natural consequence of the first two — following Jesus (destroying the works of the devil). When Moses was in the world (Egypt) his efforts delivered one slave and destroyed one Egyptian. Now, freed from the world and crucified in his flesh, he was sent back into the world (Egypt). There he was used by God to deliver a whole nation, and to destroy the whole Egyptian army in one operation. Absolutely amazing!

Deliverance

Would it not be worth forty years of testing, if afterwards we could free our country from the iron bands that grip it? Undoubtedly. Our materialistic society baulks at this, because we have become used to quick or even instant results. We live in a society where the ethos is "get the goods (or the blessings) now, and pay later". This is contrary to God's way. All creation preaches the principles of God. Death comes before resurrection. Night comes before day, the cross before the crown. Why does modern Christianity use methods and looks for results that contradict these principles?

Moses is a wonderful example of an intercessor. He changed God's mind on more than one occasion. Read in Exodus 32 how he saved a whole nation from God's wrath by his intercession. Christians have grown into a way of thinking that if they attend a few seminars, spend a day at an intercession celebration, shout at the devil and tell him that he is already defeated, then they are intercessors. How is it possible for them to be so deluded?

What was the secret of Moses' intercession? It is extremely simple. Moses had become a man who God would listen to and speak with face to face. Christians can be so busy seeking God's hand of provision that they never seek his face. But God will listen to a man who has freed himself from the world and had his character moulded in the furnace of affliction. All intercessors have this in common. Abraham was *the friend of God.* Daniel was *a man greatly beloved* of God. Praying Moses' or Daniel's prayers will not make us intercessors. God does not listen to our prayers alone; he also listens to our heart. If they do not say the same thing we would be better not to pray at all.

'Tis not enough to bend the knee
And words of prayer to say
The heart must with the mind agree
Or else we do not pray

CHAPTER 9

Daniel

In those days I Daniel was mourning three full weeks. I ate no pleasant bread, neither came flesh or wine in my mouth, neither did I anoint myself at all, till three whole weeks were fulfilled ... Then said Gabriel unto me, Fear not, Daniel: for from the first day that thou didst set thine heart to understand, and to chasten thyself before thy God, thy words were heard, and I am come for thy words ... but the prince of the kingdom of Persia withstood me twenty-one days.

Daniel 10:2-3, 12-13

Daniel is another perfect example of this process of sanctification through the three stages that Jesus outlined. Daniel was one of God's chosen people, of the royal seed, and yet found himself in Babylon. Egypt typifies the world **before** God calls us, but Babylon typifies the world **after** we have been called. Here we see God's people in captivity. It may seem strange to us that God should tell Israel not to try and fight Babylon, or to escape, but to stay there and serve it. (Jeremiah 29:4-7)

Jesus' instructions are no different from this, for he does not tell us to escape the world; on the contrary, he tells us to be in the world, and to *come under authority to the governing bodies, for God has ordained them.* Nevertheless, he did say was that we are not **of** the world. This means that our values and thinking are different from the politics, fashions, desires and dictates of the world.

In Babylon

The first thing that Daniel and his three friends did when they found themselves in Babylon was to make a decision to be different, and this difference was not just in their thinking or religion, but in their lifestyles. It is much too easy to "believe that you believe", without it affecting your lifestyle.

Daniel and his friends chose not to eat the king's meat. I am sure that the king's meat was good and wholesome, but they would have had to defile themselves by eating unclean foods such as pork, which was forbidden under the law of Moses. They chose to eat no meat at all, and instead asked for simple food, pulses, that were conducive to a life of self-denial and fasting. Daniel prayed openly three times a day. The bible clearly records that Daniel fulfilled the first stage of denying himself. He was in the world, but he made a decision to not be part of it.

A clear message

There is a very clear message which can be deduced from this. One day we will be living as kings with Jesus himself when he comes to reign on this earth; but until his kingdom comes on earth, we are instructed to live as pilgrims and aliens. A pilgrim cannot live as a king, and a king would never live as a pilgrim. It is up to us to decide which life we want to live now. Our future position when Jesus sets up his kingdom on earth rests upon that decision.

Daniel also fulfilled the second stage (crucifying the flesh), for the bible records that he fasted regularly. I do not know of any greater spiritual exercise than fasting for dealing with our old nature. It is a commandment of Jesus in his Sermon on the Mount, and one of the three activities he said must be done in secret. Daniel was also a man of much prayer, which is another of these secret activities that Jesus teaches us in Matthew 6:1-18.

True intercession

What were the consequences of coming through these two stages for Daniel? Power with God in intercession, and great revelation. The angel Gabriel was personally despatched from God to give Daniel tremendous revelations, with the message that he was greatly beloved of God. Daniel's prayer of intercession resulted in God's people returning to the promised land, their own kingdom. By this, Daniel was destroying the devil's work — undoing the work of Nebuchadnezzar, who is a type of the antichrist. It was not Daniel who fought the devil or his angels. By humbling himself with prayer and fasting, he allowed the real battle to be fought **in the heavenlies** — between angels (Michael) and devils (the prince of Persia). Daniel's humility gave a legal right for the battle to commence and to be won. It was not won by Daniel, but by spiritual powers on both sides. The battle is always the Lord's.

CHAPTER 10

Jesus

Be ye therefore perfect, even as your Father which is in heaven is perfect.

Matthew 5:48

It may seem strange that I have chosen to use Jesus as an example of this process; for why would he have to go through any process of perfection? Surely he was already perfect and sinless?

To understand the answer, we need to realise that being sinless is different from being perfect. Paul writes in his letter to the Hebrews 5:8, *Jesus, though he was a Son, learned obedience by the things which he suffered; and* ***being made perfect****, he became the author of eternal salvation.* We know that Jesus was without sin, so it is obvious that this perfection cannot be anything to do with sin. It could only concern his spiritual growth and maturity — the process of being made perfect.

Therefore, when Jesus tells us to be perfect, he cannot possibly be referring to a **sinless** life, but to a life of

obedience and maturity. A study of the life of Jesus will plainly show that he went through the very things that he asks us to go through, because it is God's way for everyone, even his own Son.

Out of Egypt

Matthew 2:14-15 records that Jesus was taken to Egypt by his parents, to fulfil the Old Testament prophecy of Hosea, *Out of Egypt have I called my son.* Hosea 11:1 is referring to Israel, and we know that God called the whole nation of Israel out of Egypt, but if we accept that Egypt typifies the world, then this process and prophecy will apply to anyone who God calls out of the world. Jesus physically came out of Egypt, and this was symbolic, but he also abandoned the world's systems entirely when he started his ministry.

Up to the time when he began his ministry, it seems that no one thought of Jesus as anything but "the carpenter's son". When he started to preach and do miracles, Mark 3:21 states that his friends said he was *beside himself*: in other words, he had gone mad. What made them say this? It was not the miracles, because madmen do not do miracles. I believe it was his new lifestyle that they thought was madness, to forsake everything and leave the world.

A new lifestyle

Personally I find that Christians will allow me a difference of opinion on many non-fundamental issues, but when I challenge them with a different **lifestyle**, this always brings opposition. It is always a greater challenge than doctrine, because lifestyle is belief in action, or proof of conviction. A strong conviction without action does not have any merit at all. When Jesus started his ministry he left all, lived entirely by faith, and preached the gospel. There is no record at all that Jesus ever mended a table or chair, or did anything to earn his own living once he had started his ministry.

Read Luke 12:13-14 for an example of Jesus' refusal to be drawn into any legal debate. He never once talked against the Roman occupation, despite its cruelty and injustice. His statement was that his kingdom was not of this world, and all his teachings and lifestyle testify to this fact. What a testimony it would be if present-day Christians would live as aliens and pilgrims in this world, and not dependent on its systems.

Jesus in the wilderness

When Jesus asks us to sit down and consider the cost, it is because he also had to count the cost himself. Why did Jesus need to be tempted in the wilderness? It is because he had the flesh, the old nature of Adam. With free will, there also comes the possibility for sin. Jesus must have had his own free will, or his prayers in Gethsemenae do not make any sense; clearly there was a battle of two wills. The devil's questions must have appealed to Jesus' flesh, or else it was no test. Look at the last temptation to see how appealing it must have been for Jesus. The devil offered him *all the kingdoms of this world and the glory of them* if he would worship him. The devil did not say "reject God". Satan does not care if we have dual worship. It is God who specifies that he alone must be worshipped.

Revelation 5:12 shows us what Jesus was given after he was obedient and had been through the cross. They are the trappings of earthly power; all the things that

Satan was offering him in the wilderness. Jesus is *worthy to receive power, and riches, and wisdom, and strength, and honour, and glory, and blessing.* These things were offered to Jesus, but without the cost of the cross. Satan was offering him nothing less than the position of antichrist. Instead of Jesus suffering and taking the sins of the whole world upon himself, Satan was giving him the alternative — to evade the cross and its suffering, and rule the world as antichrist. He wanted Jesus to persuade the whole world to worship Satan, as the antichrist will surely do. I can almost hear him taunting Jesus: "Don't be foolish, Jesus. Why should you die for these people? They always disobey God in the end anyway. Why should you die for them? They are not worth the price! Even when God restores them, it is only a matter of time before I seduce them again. History has proved it. Jesus, they are not worth it. Of course you will inherit the world if you die for them, but why go through that when you can have it **now** without the cross?"

Sweat like blood

Surely it was a great and real temptation for Jesus to be offered the things that had already been promised, immediately and without any pain. If you have any doubts at all about the severity and pressure that this put upon Jesus, then read how he prayed in Luke 22:41-44. Before he went to the cross, as he prayed to his Father *his sweat was like great drops of blood falling to the ground,* and he said, *Father, take this cup from me. My will is to refuse the cross; nevertheless your will be done.* He prayed this not once but three times. Our enemy is far too cunning to offer us something that could not tempt us. He is a master of strategy.

This battle in the wilderness is the same one that Moses faced. Only after Moses had been forty years in the wilderness did God say that he was the meekest man on earth. Jesus took forty days to overcome his flesh. Jesus and Moses both went through this process before they started their ministries.

Not for novices

How could you or I, for one moment, suppose that we were above the same test? It is presumptuous to go into the ministry before God has dealt with us. No wonder there are tragedies among God's ministers. We find men greedy for filthy lucre, or still with the lusts of the flesh submerged below the surface, ready to be exposed by Satan when it can do the most damage to God's kingdom. Self or ego is the biggest hindrance to a godly life and effective ministry.

The real ministry

After Jesus had been through the first two steps, he fulfilled the final stage in the process — his ministry which was *to destroy the works of the devil.* Just as in our other examples, it was a natural consequence. Jesus was now ready to do the will of his Father, not his own ministry or will. Only after Jesus had been baptised (which signified death to the old nature and the world) and crucified his flesh, did he start his ministry.

John 5:19 says, *Verily, verily I say unto you, The Son can do nothing of himself, but what he sees the Father do: for whatever things he does, these also the Son does likewise*. Jesus now began to destroy the works of the devil. He started to undo the process that the devil had wrought in the world. He healed the sick, fed the poor, and challenged men to be perfect as his Father in heaven was perfect. Jesus did not do anything in his own power or for his own glory.

What an example for us all, as we endeavour to be separate from this world, subdue our carnal flesh, and be a threat to the kingdom of Satan.

PART 3
The Keys

And the disciples came, and said unto him, Why speakest thou unto them in parables? He answered and said unto them, Because it is given unto you to know the mysteries of the kingdom of heaven, but to them it is not given.
For whosoever hath, to him shall be given, and he shall have more abundance: but whosoever hath not, from him shall be taken away even that he hath.
Therefore speak I to them in parables: because they seeing see not; and hearing they hear not, neither do they understand.
And in them is fulfilled the prophecy of Esaias, which saith, By hearing ye shall hear, and shall not understand; and seeing ye shall see, and shall not perceive:
For this people's heart is waxed gross, and their ears are dull of hearing, and their eyes they have closed; lest at any time they should see with their eyes, and hear with their ears, and should understand with their heart, and should be converted, and I should heal them.

Matthew 13:10-16

CHAPTER 11

God's Purpose

We have considered the cost of being a disciple of Jesus, and seen that the first part is to deny self, which means living and thinking differently than the world. This is something we have to do ourselves. God doesn't help us, because it is in our own power to do this. We can cancel a dubious newspaper or send our television back if we decide that it is hindering our walk with God. The angel Gabriel will not come to my house one night and take my television away, with a note explaining his reasons. We can and must do these things ourselves. It is not enough to quote the bible and say this world is not our home and that we are aliens, unless we live like aliens.

The second part of the cost is to take up our cross, and for our old nature to be crucified. We have seen that we cannot crucify our flesh by strength of will, because the flesh is the secret thoughts and motives of our heart, and we do not know our own hearts. Only God knows our hearts, and therefore only God can deal with our flesh. However, this does not mean that we sit passively waiting for him to do the work, for we must always be active. Nevertheless the process is indirect on our part because Christ does the actual work, so that we cannot glory in the flesh.

A two-way process

Before we look at the process of holiness and our part in it, we must understand that it is a two-way process. God also has an active part in the process of our holiness. Christianity is about change, not just forgiveness. When men or women have their sins forgiven they become **righteous**, that is, right before God, but not **holy**. This means that they now no longer have to pay the punishment for their sins, past, present, or even future. Faith in the atoning blood of Christ covers them until they receive their sinless bodies in the resurrection.

Ephesians 1:4 shows us that in one sense God does separate us to himself: *He has chosen us in him before the foundation of the world that we should be holy.* But there are also scriptures such as 1 Peter 1:15-16, *But as he which hath called you is holy, so be ye holy in all manner of conversation; because it is written, Be ye holy, for I am holy.* Here God asks **us** to be holy, and he will not do this part for us. It is this aspect of holiness that I am discussing; it means **separation from the world**. It means becoming like Christ in our very nature or character. This does not happen automatically when a person is forgiven. It is not an act of grace by God; it is a lifestyle of commitment from us. We can be forgiven instantly, but we can not become holy in an instant, and this is where so many Christians stumble. They **want** to be holy, but because no-one has explained the **process** of holiness to them, they assume they **have** become holy, and try to behave in a holy manner outwardly. This of course is not true holiness, but hypocrisy.

Many other Christians realise that despite their outward change of morality, they still have problems with their secret life. They admit that they still have anger, lust, pride, selfishness, or ego in their heart, even though they control their outward actions, and so they feel as if they are second class Christians. For twenty years I was in this second class, always feeling condemned, always covering my old nature with a moral exterior.

Obviously neither of these conditions is satisfactory, but what is the solution? It will not be difficult if we can understand two things: God's **purpose** for our lives, and the **process** he uses to bring about his purposes.

What is God's purpose?

God's purpose for mankind since Adam's fall has been to reveal his character to his fallen creation. It was exactly the same in the Old Testament, from the call of Abraham, as it is now in this present age — God is looking for a small group of people, a minority who will show to the majority his character.

I am sure this will sound ridiculous and simplistic to many Christians, because the church has assimilated the world's mentality that "big is beautiful", and that "the majority are always right". As the adverts say "How can a million housewives be wrong?" Unfortunately, very easily. In fact the majority are always wrong. Jesus gave a very honest appraisal of the situation in this world. Talking to his disciples he said in Matthew 7:13-14, *Strait is the gate and narrow is the way that leads to life, and* ***few*** *find it. Wide is the gate and broad is the way that leads to destruction, and the* ***majority*** *are on it.*

Evangelists sometimes take this verse out of context and use it to preach to sinners as a gospel message: the wide gate and the broad way is sin, the way to hell; the narrow way is grace, and the way to heaven. But this is a serious misinterpretation of scripture. The Sermon on the Mount is for **disciples**, and the very reverse is true: grace is the widest possible gate; it covers the whole world. Grace is as wide as hell itself. Jesus took away the sin of the whole world. It was nailed to the cross. The only thing that stops anyone being forgiven is the refusal to personally accept this fact. Grace is a wide gate, not a narrow one. The narrow gate and road that Jesus talked about is the narrow way of discipleship.

Israel's commission

In Deuteronomy 14:2 God spoke through Moses and told Israel, *You are a holy people unto the Lord your God, and the Lord has chosen you to be a peculiar people unto himself, above all nations that are on the earth.* This is not an isolated scripture; God had already told them many times that they were to be separate and different. Leviticus 20:24-26 reads, *But I have said unto you, ye shall inherit their land, and I will give it unto you to possess, a land flowing with milk and honey: I am the Lord your God, which have separated you from other people ... And you shall be holy unto me: for I the Lord am holy, and I have severed you from other people, that you should be mine.*

"Holy" means separate or different. How, in what sense, were they to be different, or separate? It must be that they were to be **different from the majority**. Another word used in this verse is "peculiar": *a peculiar people unto himself*, and although the word has changed its meaning in English over the centuries, it retains the same connotation of being different, distinct, or separate. If a person is different to, or separate from, the majority, they become "peculiar". When the majority become "peculiar" then the equation turns around, and those who were peculiar become normal. Those who were normal have now become the minority, and **they** are now the ones who are known as different or peculiar. So the peculiar are always the minority.

The last part of the verse says, *above all the nations that are in the earth.* Israel were to be different from all the other nations. God's purpose for his people was not to subdue the earth. It is true that he told Adam to do this before he had sinned, but **since** sin entered into the world God has never again given this commandment. God wanted a remnant who would show and declare his character as a witness to the whole world, because the world was now under God's judgement. God will never execute his judgements without there first being a witness to his holiness — salt in the earth — so that his punishment is just, and seen to be just, by angels, devils and the whole of mankind.

Israel's restrictions

God told Moses in Deuteronomy 11:24, *Wherever the soles of your feet shall tread shall be yours.* They were to conquer and subdue the land until it had peace. This verse also gives the boundaries of the land that they were to subdue, which were *from the wilderness and Lebanon, from the Euphrates, to the uttermost sea.* This is an area smaller than Great Britain. Israel had no mandate from God to conquer any other land than this. They were to show God's character to the rest of the world; they were to be a peculiar people, a nation of priests, holy unto the Lord.

Biblical history records that they failed to do this, and time and again they became entangled with the customs and idols of the surrounding nations. They could not keep themselves separate or holy. Even Levi, the tribe which God had separated for himself from within Israel, the tribe which was to be particularly "peculiar" and holy, failed miserably. The very priesthood, who came from this tribe, as soon as they were consecrated, offered *strange fire unto the Lord.*

The church's commission

I find exactly the same instructions in the New Testament for the church today, although it seems to contradict much popular modern teaching. Peter in his first letter says exactly the same things to the church that Moses told Israel: *You are a chosen generation, a royal priesthood, a holy nation, a peculiar people, that you should show forth the praises of him who has called you out of darkness into his marvellous light.* The same principles of holiness and separation must therefore apply to the church, and this is consistent with the teaching of Jesus and the apostles.

Jesus was the light, but the world did not understand or tolerate the light, and they crucified him. In other words, the light was extinguished. He told the disciples that **they** were to be light, but that they should expect the same opposition that he faced. In John 15:20 Jesus plainly tells his disciples that they were not to expect **recognition**, but rather **rejection**. *The servant is not greater than his lord. If they have persecuted me, they will also persecute you; if they have kept my sayings, they will also keep yours.*

The "great commission" given in the gospels does not tell us to take the world for Jesus. It does not ask the church to subdue the world, nor even to Christianise it. Neither does it suggest that wherever our feet tread will be ours. There is not one scripture that tells us to claim our cities for Christ; on the contrary, we are told to *shake the dust off our feet* when we leave a city that has rejected our message. If God has respect to the free will of men, so must we. If people choose to reject the gospel, that is their prerogative. Our commission is simply to give the whole world the opportunity to accept or reject the gospel.

No excuse

Mark's gospel, which seems to be the most popular quotation of the last commission, says in Chapter 16:15, *Go into all the world and tell the good news to every creature.* The church has no excuse if it does not tell every living creature of God's love and grace; but we are not politicians, and therefore we must not use lobbying, slogans, or similar methods to pressurise or manipulate people in any way, because the free will of man must always be respected. Verse 16 says, *those that believe will be saved and those that do not shall be damned.* Just a simple statement; God will add to the church such as should be saved. If people do not receive our message, Matthew 10:14 tells us to *shake the dust off our feet* and go elsewhere. The results must never be our concern. Our concern is to tell every person the good news.

Hellfire preaching

Many Christians think that the "good news" includes telling people that they are going to hell if they do not repent. Although this practice is very popular in evangelism, there is no scripture to support it.

Jesus only spoke about hell to his disciples or to those who claimed to be in the light, the Pharisees. I cannot find where Jesus ever talked about hell to the sinner. The epistles do not encourage us to preach about hell either. God wants our love from our own free will. Deciding to serve God because we want to escape hell is not the best of motives, and not the best basis for a healthy relationship. I do believe in the lake of fire, and I believe that all those who are rebellious will go there with the devil and his angels; but I am talking here of the gospel. The gospel is the good news, not the bad news. I believe that God is a good God, and he would be worth serving even if there were no rewards and no punishment.

It has often been said that there is no other reason for the existence of the church on earth except to evangelise and win the world for Christ. At face value this seems a fair appraisal, because we have been brought up on such doctrines, but there is nothing in the teachings of Jesus to support such a view. Jesus did not mention once that there would be a world-wide revival, or that the church would govern the world before his return. In fact he said the very opposite when asked by his disciples about the end times. Warning the disciples in Matthew 24:4 he said, *Take heed that no man deceive you*, and then went on to talk of deception and persecution before his return. The teaching of the apostles is no different from this. Paul in 2 Thessalonians 2:3 also says, *Let no man deceive you by any means*, exactly as Jesus had said. He then exhorts them in verse 15 to hold fast in a time when great deception and persecution is coming.

We have many doctrines and methods of evangelism, but true evangelism is a simple, natural consequence of holiness. It happens spontaneously and automatically. A holy life has its own energy to lighten the darkness. When Christians make evangelism a **cause**, and not a **consequence** as it should be, then it in fact becomes counter-productive to the true life of Christ.

The true purpose of the church

In conclusion, let me take you through a few verses in Ephesians 4; for here Paul clearly shows us God's purpose for our lives. Verse 11 lists the five ministry offices which cover all that is needed in the church. These are **apostles, prophets, evangelists, pastors and teachers.** What is the overall vision that these key people should have in their minds as they minister? The next few verses are revealing, because they tell us the purpose for which God gave these offices, and what the results should be: *for the perfecting of the saints, for the work of the ministry, for the edifying of the body of Christ.*

The results of this are: *unity of faith; knowledge of the Son of God; a perfect man; the measure of the stature of the fullness of Christ; no longer children, tossed about by every wind of doctrine.* There is nothing at all here about evangelism. The five ministries are solely to produce something mature and pure — the spotless bride. There is nothing throughout any of the epistles exhorting us to "win souls". All the instructions are about Christian lifestyle and holiness.

Natural birth

I must emphasise that I am fully behind evangelism (that is, telling the good news to every creature); but the birth of children, naturally or spiritually speaking, is a beginning, not an end. The end is to bring them to maturity. This is the focus of all New Testament teaching — to bring Christians into the very perfection of Christ.

Natural and spiritual laws both follow the same principles. When two people fall in love, children are a natural consequence of that love. A couple who are in love do not need to be told that they need to sleep together and that they ought to be producing children; nor do they need advice on the best method for achieving these results! Concentration on methods and techniques will never teach us love and compassion. Why does the church seem to need so much advice on evangelistic methods? It can only be that we don't have the one thing that matters — the relationship, the love of Christ and the compassion. If we have these, spiritual children will be a natural consequence, and we won't need any lessons, methods, or seminars. Neither will we need any motivation or exhortation. It will be the most natural thing in the world. We will actually want to do it!

CHAPTER 12

God's Process

Burn up the dross that's blackening my heart
Burn up every thing that keeps us both apart
Burn my old nature, give me a brand new start
Burn fire of God till I'm ablaze for Christ my Lord
Joanna Barratt

If God's **purpose** is for us to become a spotless mature bride for Jesus, then what is the **process** that God puts us through in order to obtain this result?

The vine

In John 15, Jesus clearly shows us a process that is fundamental and must be understood by every Christian if they are to be changed into the image of God. Those who do not understand God's process invariably find themselves blaming the devil for circumstances which God has actually brought about. They could even end up fighting God, believing that they are fighting Satan, which is a serious mistake to make. Our attitude to this process will determine what God can or cannot do in our lives.

In verse 1 Jesus says, *I am the vine, and my Father is the gardener.* This is easy to understand; but verse 2 tells us the process which God, the gardener, puts us through: *Every branch in me that does not produce fruit, he takes away.*

Two points arise from this statement. Firstly, Jesus must be talking about Christians, for only Christians are "in the vine". Secondly, it shows us that Christians can be unfruitful, and the consequences in verse 6 are serious: the unfruitful branch is *cast forth, decays, and is burned.* Christians should never find themselves in this condition. The second half of verse 2 says that *every branch that produces fruit, God prunes, that it may produce more fruit.* If we seriously consider these words of Jesus we can see that both actions from God's hand are painful. Either we are cast out and burned, or we are pruned back hard — cut back to the stump. Does it seem strange that if we please God, the gardener, and produce fruit, we are so painfully treated? This fact should not be strange to us, for the principle is a basic one in God's creation. Any gardener understands that to produce better fruit, pruning has to be carried out, and the results justify this action.

Painful pruning

The process of pruning is certainly a painful one, and there are many biblical words to describe it, such as trials, purging, or fires. There is only one reason for it in God's mind — that we should bear more fruit. In simple language this means that all Christians should grow more like their Father in character. Often the church tries to make the tree bigger, when God's purpose is to improve the **quality** of the fruit. There can be a large tree with no fruit, and there can be a small tree with much fruit. But if we want to be in God's will, we must have the same aim and purpose as God.

In this present climate where positive confession and divine health are so in favour, the idea that God himself would allow us to suffer, or that he might even be the cause of our adverse situations, is not a popular one. But I need present only a few of the many scriptures on this subject to prove the point. These scriptures will not only show us that we should expect these things, but they also tell us what our attitude ought to be towards them when they happen.

Count it all joy

In John 15:11 Jesus explained the purpose of pruning the vine. It is so *that his joy might remain in us* (that is, we do not lose it in the process) *and that our joy should be full.* We are always told to look beyond the test to the great benefit that will surely follow if we come through the test.

James starts his letter to the believers like this: *My brothers, count it all joy when you go through many tests.* A very strange way to start a letter of encouragement! But we mustn't stop there, because James goes on to give a rational explanation for his words. The very next verse begins, *Knowing this ...* Knowing the process takes the fear away. Here is the key to James' instruction. Fear of the unknown is one of the greatest fears of mankind. Our enemy Satan is paralysed and defeated if we can understand this truth, because it robs him of one of his greatest weapons: fear.

What is the knowledge that James wants to give us? *The trying of our faith produces patience. A man who is patient is complete and content.* Many Christians desire patience, but they will never obtain it, because when God starts the process which will produce patience in them, they get upset and think it's the devil attacking them. They blame the devil, and pray to God for deliverance. They pray themselves out of the very trial which will produce patience in them and make them *perfect and complete, lacking nothing*!

Leap and dance

In Luke's gospel Chapter 6:22-23, Jesus told his disciples to *leap and dance for joy.* What is amazing is that Jesus did not tell them to leap and dance when they were happy or full of the Holy Ghost, he told them the opposite. They were to *rejoice and leap for joy when men shall hate you, and separate you from their company.* This will never make sense to a Christian who believes he should expect only blessing from God, and only bad circumstances from the devil. It will be impossible to understand if they have been told that "the devil will never bother you again if you have enough faith". We can only understand these words of Jesus if we look ahead to the future results and consequences. Jesus said that we would be like the prophets of old, holy men; and *our reward would be great in heaven.*

We will always have problems if our eyes are only on the blessings we have on this earth. Jesus instructed his disciples to *lay up treasures in heaven, and not on earth.* And Paul in Colossians 3 says, *If you then be risen with Christ, seek those things which are above, where*

Christ sits on the right hand of God. Set your affection on things above, not on things on the earth.

Working for our good

Romans 8:28 is a very popular and much used verse, and in it we see exactly the same principle. Paul says that *all things work together for our good.* He does not say that all things **are** good. Persecution is not good. Sickness, pain, trials and misunderstandings are not in themselves good. Paul is saying that we should look beyond the circumstances to the future benefits, and he is reminding us that even the bad things are working towards a good purpose in our lives: that we will be *conformed to the image of his Son.* This is the *fruit that endures* — the eternal character of God. Paul finishes this chapter with the consolation that *neither death, nor life, nor angels, nor principalities, nor powers, nor things present, nor things to come, nor height, nor depth, nor any other creature, nor tribulation, nor distress, nor persecution, nor famine, nor nakedness, nor peril, nor sword, shall be able to separate us from the love of God.* Paul claims that **this** is what makes us *more than conquerors* — not that we escape trials and purgings, but that they are beneficial instead of detrimental. We can have a victorious attitude in our trials, simply because we see the future benefits.

An unusual promise

Paul, in his second letter to Timothy, Chapter 3:10-11, says something about his own lifestyle which is compatible with this view of God's process in our lives. Paul's victory is not that he was protected from trials and suffering, but that he *endured to the end.* He talks of *longsuffering, charity, patience, persecutions, and afflictions.* These, then, are the marks of a true follower. Jesus said, *Beware when all men speak well of you; that is the sign of a false prophet.* Paul reminds Timothy of a certain fact. We could almost call it a promise: *All who live godly in Christ Jesus shall suffer persecution.*

It is easy to see why this should be so. How could true holiness ever be acceptable to an *evil and adulterous generation*, a dark world? Light will either shine and challenge the darkness, or be extinguished, because the world hates it and cannot understand it.

Peter's change of attitude

Peter, when faced with persecution at the trial of Jesus, denied that he ever knew him. By this he proved that he did not believe the cross was necessary, and that he was not prepared for any adversity. On the contrary, Peter and the other apostles were looking for Jesus to *restore the kingdom to Israel* at that time, and Peter even resorted to violence at the arrest of Jesus in the garden of Gethsemenae.

In his first letter, Peter shows us that his attitude towards suffering and trials had radically changed. He could hardly have come to a more opposite point of view. Let me quote his own words in 1 Peter 4:12. *Beloved, do not think it strange at the fiery trial that is to test you, as though some strange thing has happened to you.* Peter is telling us to expect fiery trials as something normal; and the next verse, as with all our examples, looks to the future as a reason to rejoice in those trials: *But rejoice, that you are a partaker of Christ's sufferings;*

that when his glory shall be revealed, you may be glad also with exceeding joy.

We have to conclude that Peter's new attitude was one of maturity. The change is too radical and obvious to ignore. The Christian life and process is no different for modern Christians. Peter denied Christ **because he didn't want the cross**. There are only two options — either we deny ourselves or we deny Christ. This seems too drastic a statement; but we are all moving in one of these two directions, and eventually we will arrive at one of the conclusions.

A strange benediction

James begins his letter by asking us to *count our trials all joy*, but Peter ends his first letter in Chapter 5:10 with a similar exhortation — a benediction that I have yet to hear in any church. *But the God of all grace, who has called us unto his eternal glory by Jesus Christ,* ***after that you have suffered a while****, make you perfect, establish, strengthen, settle you.* This process (suffering for a while) is what we should be now expecting as Christians, and the results we should expect from our trials are exactly the same as we have seen in other scriptures. What a glorious list this is: perfect, settled, immovable, and strengthened! It should inspire us to leap into the fire and say, "God, burn up the dross in my life"! How many times do Christians lay themselves on God's sacrificial altar, believing that they have surrendered all, only to jump off when God lights the fire underneath us!

Laying ourselves on God's altar could even be a self-righteous show of the flesh, an act that is pleasing to our old nature, unless we are willing to stay on it and endure the fire. Praying ourselves out of our trials only proves that we are unwilling to surrender anything that costs or is painful to us.

Following Paul

In Philippians 3:17 Paul exhorts us to be his followers. We need to read the context of his words so that we understand his meaning: Verse 7 says, *What things were gain to me, those I counted loss for Christ, and I count all things but loss for the excellency of the knowledge of Christ Jesus my Lord: for whom I have suffered the loss of all things, and do count them but dung, that I may win Christ, and be found in him, not having my own righteousness, which is of the law, but that which is through the faith of Christ, the righteousness which is of God through faith:*

That I may know him, and the power of his resurrection, ***and the fellowship of his sufferings****, being made conformable unto his death; if by any means I might attain unto the resurrection of the dead.*

There are many scriptures which agree with the few that I have quoted here. We have seen that the process of purging or pruning is the natural, and indeed the only, way to produce healthy growth and good fruit.

Going for gold

Gold is a precious metal and beautiful to look upon. The tabernacle and temple, where God dwelt with his people, were both full of gold. Gold speaks of God's glory, his character or very essence, and so it needs to be pure. Gold is not naturally pure; it needs to go through a process of refining. It is placed in a crucible and put into a furnace. The gold melts, and the impurities (dross) float to the top and are removed. This process is repeated until there are no more impurities in the gold, and only then is it left to cool and harden so it can be used.

This is exactly the process which God has to put us through, if we want to be purified. There is simply no other way. The weaknesses in our character cannot be dealt with until they are brought to the surface.

Being exposed

God can not and will not just miraculously remove the things that lie hidden deep in our heart. Moreover, God will not deal with imperfections in our character until we admit that we have those imperfections in us. Unless the pressures and heat come upon us, our impurities can remain hidden even from ourselves. When we are exposed, it is very painful and embarrassing, because when our weaknesses surface they become apparent not only to ourselves, but to others!

Often we find it hard to accept this and blame the circumstances for our behaviour; but the circumstances, far from being the cause of "out of character" behaviour, only reveal to us our real character, the real person underneath. Nothing can come out of a man that is not already within him. The pressure and heat of trials and tribulations only serve to bring the dross to the surface; and this is a **good** thing. If we are humbled then surely this is good, for humility is the very attitude that God requires. I am convinced that God will never deal with anything in our life which we are unwilling to admit is there.

Unfortunately, there is an alternative to the process of purification. We can polish the surface of the gold until it shines, and it will certainly reflect the light. But if we apply this practice to our lives, the impurities remain hidden from us and from those who observe us. Only God knows the truth in our hearts. I would fail in my role as a minister of the gospel if I did not say that "polishing the surface" is a foolish thing to do. It may be sufficient for this life, but the bible warns us that *every man's work will eventually be tried by fire* and all will be revealed. I would suggest that it is far better to be humbled in this life, and be of use to God, than to wait for the judgement of the saints and *suffer loss.*

Tried by fire

Paul, in 2 Corinthians 5:10, says, *For we must all appear before the judgement seat of Christ; that everyone may receive the things done in his body, according to that which he has done, whether it be good or bad*; and in 1 Corinthians 3:12, *Now if any man build upon this foundation gold, silver, precious stones, wood, hay, stubble; Every man's work will be manifest: for the day shall declare it, because* ***it will be revealed by fire****; and the fire shall try every man's work of what sort it is. If any man's works endure that he has built, he shall receive a reward. If any man's work shall be burned, he shall suffer loss: but he himself shall be saved; yet so as by fire.* (If we are in any doubt, Paul is clearly talking about Christians, because he says that they will be saved. He could never say this to people who do not know God.)

Listen to what the Spirit is saying to the churches, especially to those who feel they are *rich and increased with goods*, those who are *in need of nothing* materially or spiritually. Certainly, much of the church in materialistic societies seem to have such an attitude. Revelation 3:18 says, *I counsel you to buy of me gold tried in the fire, that you may be rich; and white clothing, that you may be clothed, and that the shame of your nakedness does not appear; and anoint your eyes with eye salve, that you may see. He that has ears to hear, let him hear.*

CHAPTER 13

God's Character

What must we do to become mature and holy? What are the keys? Why do some Christians continue to change and grow, while others only stagnate and shrink? Is holiness a hit-and-miss affair, or are there clear instructions laid out in the word of God?

I am going to look at this great mystery of holiness, the deep and unfathomable process whereby a person changes in their very motives and root actions. Firstly, allow me to share some of the principles which lie behind the instructions of Jesus. It is much easier to be obedient when we have understanding. There is no benefit in having blind faith, if all we need is natural sight.

The two-sided coin

If we are going to seek the character of God, then it is essential that we first ask ourselves if we really know and understand what his character is like. To help us answer this question, let me share a principle that can apply to all our studies.

I have found that few Christians know this simple fact: **Truth can never come from a single statement.**

Our western thinking is based on systematic logic, single statements of truth. An example of this could be the statement, "This water is hot." Therefore, according to our systematic logic, the water is not cold. There are only two alternatives, hot or cold, and the two cannot both be true. One is the truth, and the other must therefore be a lie.

But what if the water is lukewarm? That's a mixture, or both hot **and** cold. And who decides what is "hot" anyway? It's all relative; 70 degrees is hot compared to 40 degrees, but tepid compared to 100 degrees! In the end we find that our western "absolute facts" are based on arbitrary designations of science, grammar or logic We say this is blue, therefore it is not green; this is a tree, so it's not a bush; but they are all man-made qualifications and explanations, and **we make a serious mistake in applying the same methods to knowing God.**

We try to know God by science and logic instead of by relationship; we define and qualify his attributes and characteristics: he is like this, so he is not like that. Relationship never needs to know "facts"; relationship only demands the **experience** of knowing a **person**.

Western mentality

The problem with our western thinking is that the bible was not written with western mentality. Neither was it written with eastern or middle-eastern mentality. The bible tells us clearly that it was written *as men were instructed by the Holy Ghost.* So the bible is the thinking of **God**. The inspiration came from the Holy Ghost. We must not allow ourselves to forget this fact, otherwise we will not seek for revelation from the Holy Ghost. It is so easy to spend our time dissecting the Greek or Hebrew and become pseudo-scholars, and to be robbed of spiritual food. The bible does not need understanding and reasoning; it needs **revelation**. Of course there are scholars who spend all their lives studying the ancient manuscripts, and I am not criticising them. I am saying that we need the Person who wrote the bible to reveal the bible to us.

Apparent contradictions

I must now go further, and say that not only does truth sometimes have two sides, it always contains an apparent contradiction. I say "apparent" because the opposites are only two sides of the same truth and can co-exist perfectly together. Maybe a very simple illustration will help our understanding of this claim.

If I held a coin up to a you so that the head was facing you, it is obvious you would not see the tail. I, on the opposite side, would see the tail and not the head. If I asked what was on the coin we would both declare the side we could see and **we would both be correct, even though we were in disagreement.** To understand the truth, neither you nor I would have to change or modify the **coin** (our example of the truth); we would only have to change our **position**.

I can almost hear some people saying that this is nothing more than a plea for compromise. Am I suggesting that there is no absolute truth, and that everything is relative? Am I watering down the truth? On the contrary, I am making a plea for the opposite of compromise. My illustration tells us that absolutes **do** exist, and that truth can never, and will never, change. But **I must be able to see both sides if I am to fully understand the truth.**

What does God say?

Let God speak for himself. Whenever God declared his own character, he used two statements that seem contradictory. In the ten commandments, Exodus 20:5 states: *The Lord your God is a jealous God, visiting the iniquity of the fathers upon the children unto the third and forth generation of them that hate me...*

This first statement shows that God is a fearful judge; but the statement continues in verse 6, *... and showing mercy unto thousands of them that love me and keep my commandments.* Here is a forgiving, merciful father. Which statement tells us the real character of God? Is our God a jealous, fearful avenger, or is he a loving, forgiving, merciful, pardoning God?

God's glory

When Moses asked God to reveal himself and show him his glory, God hid Moses in a cleft of a rock and declared his character. What did God say about himself? He said exactly the same as in the ten commandments — he declared **the two sides to his character**. Exodus 34:6-7 — *The Lord, the Lord, merciful and gracious, longsuffering, and abundant in goodness and truth; keeping mercy for thousands, forgiving iniquity and transgression and sin...* Here is the loving, forgiving and understanding God; but he continues with the opposite picture: *... and that will by no means clear the guilty: visiting the iniquity of the fathers upon the children, and* *upon the children's children, unto the third and to the fourth generation.*

Which is the true character of God? Our systematic logic will tell us it is either one or the other; it cannot be both. But the truth of God's character is **both** statements.

The pendulum

Let me remind you of our principle: **truth can never come from a single statement.** The danger comes when only one side of God's character is preached to the exclusion of the other. Only the **whole** truth sets us free. Before a witness is allowed to give evidence in a court of law, they are asked to make the following oath: "I swear by Almighty God to tell the truth, the whole truth, and nothing but the truth". Why does the law not just require "the truth"? Because even the law understands that a single statement, or one side of the truth, is not enough; it needs the whole truth; more than just one statement, in order to get a true assessment of the facts.

Ministers of the gospel must preach that God is loving and forgiving, and that he wants to bless us. They must also preach that he is a fearful judge, and that we will have to give an account for every idle word uttered: that suffering, as well as blessing, is an integral part of the Christian life. Failure to do this will bring about a distorted gospel and slander the true character of God. This principle is consistent throughout the bible, and our understanding of it will make all the difference to our comprehension of God's word.

CHAPTER 14

Two Natures

In John's first letter to the church, Chapter 1:8 reads, ***If we say that we have no sin, we deceive ourselves,*** *and the truth is not in us.* John is very definitely addressing Christian believers. He is addressing those who have repented and received the forgiveness of God. It would be wonderful if the atonement made us sinless, but as any honest believer knows, this is not the case. We are forgiven, and righteous (right with God), and we are no longer **accountable** for our sins, because the atonement is an eternal sacrifice. Even the sins we will commit in future are paid for in full; but we are not and never will be sinless while we remain in our mortal bodies.

Christians still sin

Sin is anything less than perfection — that is, anything less than the perfect will of God. A lustful thought, anger without reason, an exaggeration of the facts that become a lie; we cannot live one day without sinning. Paul reassures us that there is no more condemnation from God, nor any power of accusation from Satan, because the price has been paid for us in advance, and we are freed to serve God.

Knowing that this letter is addressed to believers makes verse 9 very interesting. John says, *If we confess our sins, God is faithful and just to forgive us our sins, and to cleanse us from all unrighteousness.* Let us suppose that John had been addressing unbelievers. He would have written differently, and said, "God is merciful and gracious", because mercy and grace are what is needed for our sins to be forgiven. Instead, John uses the words "faithful and just". What do faithfulness and justice have to do with forgiveness? The answer is: absolutely nothing! Christians have already received mercy and grace, and their forgiveness is complete, so what is John trying to tell us by using these words? He is saying that if we are honest to admit that we still sin, then God is **faithful and just to keep his promise**. God will continue to forgive us, and we should have no further problem with condemnation.

More evidence

It is not just one scripture in John which convinces me of this; many other scriptures, for example in Paul's letters to the Galatians and Romans, tell us exactly the same thing. But I should not need Paul to reveal this condition to me, nor should I need any other scriptures to convince me of the fact that I still sin. I need look no further than my own heart and my daily life. Even though I am hungering and thirsting for righteousness, and even though I know I have grown over the years, I can say the same as Paul when he confessed to the church in Romans 8:19, *For the good that I want to do, I do not do; but the evil I don't want to do, I find myself doing.* I still have this inner conflict, after many years, but I am completely free from any condemnation because God is faithful and just to his word, and his Son Jesus is ever interceding for me at the Father's right hand.

Christians cannot sin

In the same letter of John, just thirty-five verses after our first statement that Christians cannot live without sinning, Chapter 3:6 says, *Whoever abides in Jesus* ***does not sin****: whoever sins has not seen him, neither have they known him*; and in verse 9, *Whoever is born of God* ***does not commit sin****; for his seed remains in him: and* ***he cannot sin****, because he is born of God.*

John has just clearly told us in chapter 1 that Christians still commit sin, and yet now we have a clear statement that a Christian does not sin, and, even more surprisingly, **cannot** sin.

A subtle approach

Once again, we see the principle I outlined in the previous chapter being applied by John: there is always more than one side to truth. Truth always contains opposites and contradictions. If we do not recognise this principle, we have to conclude that one of John's statements is true and the other is false. This is in effect what many Christians do.

However, they cannot confess this outright, because they profess to believe that the bible is all the inspired word of God, and therefore there cannot be any falsehood or contradictions in it. So they are forced to take a more subtle approach: they pick out the side of the truth that they find easier to agree with, and then they justify the existence of the scriptures that put the opposite side by saying, "Well, I know that John **said** that, but what he really **meant** was ..." and they have to try and fit the awkward statement into one of their "proven doctrines" to justify themselves. Alternatively they may say that "we must not take the dead letter of the word, but understand the spirit of what the writer was trying to tell us"; and that way give themselves a licence to make the scriptures say almost whatever they want them to say, so they don't offend their doctrines.

I am not saying this in order to be critical or sarcastic in any way, but because I realise the difficulty that people face when they believe that truth can be contained in a single statement. I am just trying to demonstrate the problems that arise from this belief.

No reconciliation

How can we reconcile two opposite statements in the bible? We can not, and we certainly should not. Both opposing statements will always stand up perfectly well on their own without any need for "reconciliation". There is always an answer if we look at the coin as a whole and not the "contradiction" of the two sides.

The answer to John's two statements is a simple one, once we can accept that they are **both** true statements in themselves. The answer is that **each statement is referring to a different nature or character**. A Christian is a person who has two completely different characters. The statements of John fit perfectly, because one of these characters **cannot sin**, and the other one **cannot cease from sin**. Let us look at these two characters in detail so that we are in no doubt as to the biblical truth of this.

The old nature, or character, is also known as the **Adamic** nature, because it began with Adam's sin. Every Christian knows that Adam was created without sin, but many do not realise that **he was also created without a conscience**.

The tree of conscience

This is obvious when we consider that the tree which God forbade Adam to eat was called *the tree of the knowledge of good and evil.* "The knowledge of good and evil" is a perfect definition of the word "conscience"; the two terms are interchangeable. Adam did not have a conscience, which means he did not have a moral choice. Morality can only come from a knowledge of what is good and what is evil. God did not want Adam to know evil **or good**, because he forbade him access to the tree, the means of obtaining this information. Adam's choice was purely one of obedience or disobedience, and nothing at all to do with his definitions of what was good and evil.

Obedience

It is not often understood that obedience and disobedience are nothing to do with conscience, morality, good and evil, or right and wrong. Adam was told to be obedient. But he was not being obedient because he knew it was "right" or "moral" or "good" to be obedient, or because his conscience told him to do so. Likewise, when he was disobedient, he was not doing something which he knew was wrong or evil. Adam had no moral "value system" of what was right and what was wrong. All he had was God's command, "Obey, don't disobey"; no reasons why, no morality at all. Obedience is a separate issue from morality and conscience.

I am at pains to emphasise this point because **true Christianity is not to do with morals and conscience**. That's the wrong tree — the tree of knowledge of good and evil. Christianity is to do with access to the tree of life, obedience, and submission to God's will. Obedience gave Adam access to the tree of life; but when he ate of the tree of knowledge of good and evil he was cut off from the tree of life. Conscience, the knowledge of good and evil, is actually destructive to Christianity. It gets in the way of simple obedience, because when a person has a knowledge of good and evil, there is no guarantee that their definition of what is good and what is evil will agree with what God considers good or evil. Romans 5:18-19 says that *because of one man's **disobedience,** sin came upon every man*. This means that we are born sinners. It does not say that we are born perfect and then begin to sin at some later time when we understand. It is the very character that we are born with, and it is our inheritance from our father in the flesh, Adam.

Reproduction

A clear teaching throughout the bible is that **everything God created reproduces its own kind**. Apple trees produce apples, dogs produce dogs, and if two sinners have a child, they can produce no less or more than they are themselves — a baby sinner! I suppose that this is not very palatable to our self-image; however, we must realise that it was Adam's sin, not ours, that caused this situation. We only inherit this sin by birth. (I must point out that we also sin by choice, but this is another matter.)

Sin is natural

Any parent will confirm that a child does not need lessons in how to be greedy, selfish, or stubborn. These things all come naturally! What we do have to teach our children is that they must be **un**selfish and obedient. It needs chastisement to implement the necessary changes. This is becoming less and less fashionable in our humanistic society, and we are reaping the consequences of a generation of parents who thought that their children would "find their own level" of behaviour without any need for clear guidance and discipline. From our first instruction and discipline as a child, we learn to control this Adamic nature by making laws, and penalties for breaking those laws.

Covetousness

I would like to use covetousness as an example. Covetousness is the desire for something which does not belong to us. It is natural to be covetous. Many people would steal if there was no law, no punishment, and no shame attached to the offence. It would certainly be a much greater temptation.

Covetousness is common to man, and no-one is free from it. Society helps to curtail this trait in our character by creating laws and penalties. Often it is simply the fear of being found out that stops a person stealing, or committing adultery, or fulfilling any other desire of the flesh.

If what I have written seems judgmental and hard on human nature, then I must refer you to scripture and to the list that Paul gives of "the works of the flesh" (which is the same as the old nature). Galatians 5:19-21 says, *Now the works of the flesh are manifest, which are these: adultery, fornication, uncleanness, sensuality, idolatry, sorcery, enmities, strife, jealousy, outbursts of anger, disputes, dissensions, factions, envying, drunkenness, partying.* To accept that we still have the old nature is to accept that we have the potential for everything on Paul's list.

In our hearts

The **works** are in our heart and character, but the **manifestation** is in our outward actions. A person may control their actions, but it matters little to God if the "work" is still in the heart, because it is always the heart that God judges. Unfortunately, many Christians still try to control this old nature with their will. This is not the answer. Strong will can never change our character; it can only suppress the things that we are embarrassed to manifest outwardly. **Self can never change self**.

We may succeed in controlling our outward actions, as much as is possible, and assume that our heart is pure and that we are holy in character. But this will not solve the problem, because self will still be in the heart, and that has not been controlled.

The bible gives only one answer to dealing with our self life: it has to die, for it can never be controlled or purified. If we forget about the inward and judge ourselves on our outward actions, this is hypocrisy, which is the sin of the Pharisees.

The other extreme is people who are honest with themselves, and realise that their secret life is far from holy. Naturally this makes them feel condemned. For twenty years I fell into this second category. Although I was very good at deceiving other people, I did not like to deceive myself, and so I felt a second-class Christian. I was never free from guilt. I would pray and ask God to give me a strong will so that I could overcome my desires and have power over my pride, selfishness, and lust; but I never did receive the power to master these secret desires.

The new nature

After twenty years of struggle it dawned on me that God does not repair old natures; he gives us a new one. I had always known that the bible talks of a new birth, but I did not have a personal revelation of it.

If, when I was born of the flesh, I inherited the character of Adam, it is obvious that when I was born again of the Spirit, I inherited the character of Christ. What a different nature this is! Paul tells us about it in Galatians 5:22, and he calls it the "fruit of the Spirit": *The fruit of the Spirit is love, joy, peace, longsuffering, gentleness, goodness, faith, meekness, temperance; against such there is no law.* This character is in everyone who is born of God. It is impossible for us to not inherit this character if God is our Father.

The two trees

Now we should understand the answer to the two opposing statements that John made. The old Adamic nature can not be redeemed. It is fallen and always will be. As Jesus says in Matthew 7:18, *A corrupt tree cannot produce good fruit.* The Adamic nature is a bad tree and it will always sin. This of course is the bad news, but the good news is this: God, through Jesus, gives us his own nature. Now this is a different tree. It is not the tree of the knowledge of good and evil, but the tree of life, and it is perfect and cannot sin. Jesus also said in the same verse that *a good tree cannot produce bad fruit.*

A simple solution

Paul says in Romans 8 verse 2, *For the law of the Spirit of life in Christ Jesus has made me free from the law of sin and death.* These are the two laws that govern our two natures. Such a simple answer and so freeing — and yet from my observation I honestly feel that the majority of Christians spend most of their efforts trying to control the nature of Adam, believing that it can be improved or controlled, instead of forgetting about it and concentrating on feeding their new nature.

Walk in the spirit

Paul's teaching in Galatians 5:16 is that *if we walk in the spirit* (our new nature), *we will not fulfil the lusts of the flesh* (our old nature). Notice that he does not say that for Christians the lusts of the flesh just disappear. He says we do not *fulfil* them. What does this mean? The next verse shows us that there is a daily battle: *For the flesh lusts against the spirit, and the spirit against the flesh: and these are contrary one to another: so you cannot do the things that you want.*

If a person accepts the simple truth that **whichever nature we walk in will eventually manifest in our**

outward lifestyle, then it follows that we can only walk in the nature that we cultivate and feed. This is the secret to a carefree, holy life — dealing with the roots. We must starve the old nature and feed the new nature. Our behaviour will be a natural consequence of this without any need to strive or exercise strength of will.

Imagine a father teaching his children about growth by instructing them to try and stretch and to concentrate and make every effort. We could not imagine any father would be so naive. All he has to do is feed the child each day, and the growth will take care of itself. Unfortunately, many Christians are striving to grow spiritually, making every effort to be holy and mature, when all they need is the daily spiritual food which is the very thing they are neglecting! This is sad enough; but not only are they neglecting to feed the new nature, they also continue to feed the old nature

Over the years they do learn more doctrines; they learn new formulas, and methods for power and for fulfilling their own wants — but they never grow in character like their heavenly Father.

Feeding the old nature

The things that feed our old nature may seem obvious to many Christians — reading pornography, for example. However, we can become so used to our daily lifestyles, that we are not always aware of how much we may be unconsciously feeding the old nature every day. Let me take something that is not sinful of itself, like a newspaper. There is obviously a great range from obscene to good reading, but the majority of daily news is the reporting of evil, scandal, criticism, rumours or just plain lies. It is certainly always politically biased, and one paper alone can never possibly give the reader the truth. In any case, why would a Christian want to read day after day about murder, rape, political wranglings and immoral escapades, when the bible tells us in Philippians 4:8 to *think on these things: whatsoever things are true, honest, just, pure, lovely, and a good report*? These qualities do not often find their way into the newspapers!

Media influence

On the television the soap operas are based on people's insatiable desire for gossip and scandal. Television is the greatest propaganda machine this world has ever known. It changes the mindset of whole continents, and it is extremely subtle, because it works on repetition and over many years. Because of the mass media, whole continents now see the same advertising, the same views, and the same standards, and we lose our reference for what is correct in God's eyes.

Whole communities are being programmed at the same time, and unfortunately the same thing is happening in the church, as strange doctrines are being presented simultaneously to Christians throughout the world using the modern media. The world has invaded many areas of the modern church, because the ministers and the congregations have been feeding their old natures. They have believed that self can be compatible with the mind of Christ, and slowly the gospel has been corrupted and become reasonable, instead of an offence and a sword.

I have singled out the media as only one example; but if we evaluate the time we spend doing worldly things (I say again, not **sinful** things) against the time we spend actively feeding the new nature, it is not surprising that the moral standards of Christians have declined in the same proportion as the world's. If the church had maintained its standards over the past one hundred years, the gap between the world and the church would be so wide that it would bring ridicule and persecution — the very effect that Jesus said the cross would have in a society.

Stop trying

I want to end this chapter by highlighting a problem that many Christians have when they are challenged with the demands of holiness. They are willing to admit that they still have a covetous or lustful thought life, or that they are selfish, or find it hard to forgive their enemies. The problem, as they see it, is that they do not have a strong will. If only they had more will power, they think, they would be able to overcome these secret faults.

I believe the devil is very happy with this diagnosis — in fact I believe he suggested it to them in the first place. He will encourage the Christian with thoughts such as: "Try harder, God will help you", or, "Ask God to give you a stronger will". I do not believe the devil is even worried when you pray to God, if you are asking for something that God cannot give you. The devil knows that your efforts to be holy will only make you proud, and condemning of others, or, if you fail, condemn you. Either way he is pleased because he has masked the true way to holiness.

I am going to share in the next chapter what I believe and have experienced in my own life, and seen in countless others: the simple fact that **you do not need a strong will to be holy**. I am not saying that cultivating a strong will is a bad thing to do. It is good to be disciplined. What I am saying is that our will is not the root of the problem, and God's desire is always that we deal with the roots. Any other method will always be counterproductive to the real life that God has planned for us.

CHAPTER 15

All in the Mind

This I say therefore, and testify in the Lord, that from now on you walk not as other people walk, in the vanity of their mind, having the understanding darkened, being alienated from the life of God through their ignorance, because of the blindness of their heart; who being past feeling have given themselves over to lasciviousness, to work all uncleanness with greediness. But you have not so learned of Christ; if so be that you have heard him, and have been taught by him, as the truth is in Jesus: that you put off concerning the former conversation the old man, which is corrupt according to deceitful lusts; and ***be renewed in the spirit of your mind.***

Ephesians 4:17-23

If a Christian does not need a strong will to change his desires and motives, or to control his ambitions and lusts, then what does he need? One thing is certain: our natural character will not change of itself. Self needs death by crucifixion in order for the nature of Jesus to reign in our bodies, so that we can manifest the fruit of the Spirit, and not the works of the flesh. I believe that the secret is not in our **will** but in our **mind**. A change of **action** comes from a change of **attitude**.

Who needs a strong will?

Romans 7 verses 15-21 shows the battle that we all have with our two natures. In verse 19 Paul says, *For the good that I want to do, I don't do; but the evil which I don't want to do, that I do.* If strong will could make a person holy in their secret life, I am convinced Paul would have achieved it, and would not have needed to make this confession. If anyone could discipline himself by will power it was Paul the Pharisee, who was educated according to the strict letter of the law. But he has to confess that he could never do it.

Paul then says in verse 22 and 23 that in his new nature he loves God's law, but there is another law in action in his old nature which fights against the law of his mind. Verse 25 concludes: *with my **mind** I serve the law of God, but with my flesh the law of sin.*

It starts in the mind

It is not easy to accept that holiness starts in the mind, but it is the secret to true holiness — and a guard against self-righteousness, because whenever we succeed in controlling our outward actions by will power, we are in danger of becoming self-righteous and self-sufficient; self becomes exalted.

Most people accept that we have a conscious and a subconscious mind. There is a verse in Hebrews 4:12

that will help us to clarify this distinction. *For the word of God is alive, and powerful, and sharper than any two-edged sword, piercing even to the dividing asunder of soul and spirit, and of the joints and the marrow, and is a discerner of the thoughts and intents of the heart.*

Soul and spirit

There are three divisions that the word of God makes, which Christians find very difficult to understand. The first is the division *between soul and spirit.* How many debates have raged over the years between what is of the soul and what is of the spirit! Even after centuries of doctrinal investigation, the division is no more clear to the average believer.

Joints and marrow

The second division is *between the joints and the marrow.* What a strange division! When we want to get to the bottom of something we often say "Let's get to the bones of the matter", and we mean that we will strip away all that covers the truth. But the word of God can go deeper than this, for when we have stripped everything away to the very skeleton, there are still things that we cannot see. The marrow is inside the bone itself. These first two examples show us the principle, but it is the third example that concerns us here.

Thoughts and intents

The word of God can decide between the **thoughts** and **intents** of the heart. This means that there is a difference between **what we think consciously** and **what our motives, or intents, really are**, in our subconscious thinking. This is a vital difference, and one which we must understand if we are to grow in holiness.

Brain or heart

It is important that we understand the difference between the brain and the heart. I realise that there are many opinions on this subject. Often the differences of opinion are really only to do with terms and definitions, and the way we explain things based on our own background knowledge. Everyone comes from a different angle. It is necessary therefore for you to first understand my definitions, so that you can follow my arguments.

I believe that the brain is only physical, and as such is simply the biological computer of the body. This means that it cannot think for itself. It has to be programmed. The thinking, or programming, therefore comes from our spirit, the non-physical part of us. This is where our motives, ambitions, lusts, and emotions originate.

Conscious or subconscious

I now want to distinguish between conscious and subconscious thought, and I believe it is easy to do this from the bible. (I should make clear the obvious fact that flesh and spirit are connected, and therefore they often work together as one, so although my distinctions are simplistic to help our understanding, I realise much more explanation is needed to fully explore these themes).

When the bible talks about "the mind" I believe it is always referring to our self-aware, conscious thinking. For example, Paul in Philippians encourages us to *think on these things: whatsoever things are true, whatsoever things are honest, whatsoever things are just, whatsoever things are pure, whatsoever things are lovely.* We are obviously conscious of what we are thinking when we obey Paul's instructions.

The heart

Whenever the bible talks about "the heart", it is referring to the centre of us, our very roots, our **subconscious** thinking. This is where our hidden desires and ulterior motives lie, and this is also the deceitful part of us — the part that our husband, wife, boss, or minister does not know. It is even hidden from us.

We all know **what** we think, but we can never be sure **why** we think it. If ever you feel that your motives are pure and that you know yourself, then meditate on the words of Jeremiah 17:9 — *The heart is deceitful above all things, and desperately wicked: who can know it?* The heart is so deceitful that it will deceive us into thinking that it is pure! David asked God to test his heart (not his mind) and see if there was any wicked way in it. This suggests that he did not know his own heart. Study the scriptures for yourself and you will find that the heart is always where our motives and desires originate.

I am what I think

Everyone knows that what we eat is assimilated into our physical body, and so we accept the phrase that "we are what we eat". But few people realise that there is a spiritual parallel: "we are what we think" spiritually. I am not talking here about "positive confession", which teaches that we can become what we speak, what we would like to be. That is brainwashing, often tantamount to telling lies, and it has its roots in the occult. Trying to change physical and outward circumstances by the power of positive thinking (creating our own reality) is a very dangerous practice. However, this must not frighten us away from the true understanding of what it means to renew our minds. Proverbs 23:7 says that *as a man thinks in his heart, so is that man.* It is saying that what a man thinks in his **heart** — his subconscious motives and desires — is the real man, and not what he thinks in his **head** (his conscious thinking). We often think, in our head, that we are what we would like to be; but God always sees our heart. I can be no more or less a person than I am in my heart

Outward holiness

The first two verses of Romans chapter 12 will help us further to see how important a role the mind plays in the process of holiness. Verse 1 says that we should *present our bodies a living sacrifice, holy, acceptable unto God, which is our reasonable service.* The verse mentions the word "holy", but Paul is only referring here to what we could call outward holiness, because he says "present your **bodies**". Outward holiness is what the Pharisees had — the **outward** observance of the law, of holiness, of separation from the world.

It is important for us to realise that there is nothing wrong with this if it is matched by inward holiness. Jesus never criticised the Pharisees for their outward actions. He criticised them for the hypocrisy of being holy outwardly, and unclean, covetous and self-righteous inwardly. We need to be holy both inwardly and outwardly if we are to be real Christians.

The house

Paul does not say that our mind or our spirit should be a sacrifice, but our bodies Our bodies are only the house where our real, spiritual self lives. He is talking about how we present ourselves to the world — our outward holiness. Paul says a strange thing here: it is *your reasonable service.* "Reasonable" seems to be such a weak, compromising word — nothing special. Surely Paul should have said "it is our absolute duty", or some other strong phrase?

Only reasonable

I have two reasons why outward holiness is only "reasonable", only to be expected. The first is that **the hypocrites can do this**. It is not too difficult with a strong will to control our **outward** behaviour — for example, to not steal or blaspheme, to control our temper and be moral in our outward conduct, to fast and pray and give to the poor. All of these examples are only our outward behaviour, and to be expected of anyone who claims to be a Christian. Even the Pharisees in Jesus' day did all of these things; yet Jesus called them the devil's children.

If we do all these moral acts, we must not expect any praise or reward from God. It is only reasonable that people who call themselves Christians should live like this, once they are in the light and know God personally. If they are God's children, it is only reasonable that they should reflect his character in their outward behaviour.

The second reason that outward holiness is only reasonable is that **even non-Christians expect an outward standard of holiness from Christians**. When a person says that they have become a Christian, people immediately begin to look at their outward behaviour to see if their actions match their words. If they see a Christian take a pencil home from work, they will immediately say, "That's stealing — I thought Christians didn't steal". It doesn't matter if everyone else in the company takes pencils home — they expect a higher moral standard from a Christian.

A bad witness

Often Christians will justify their actions when they are accused and say, "We aren't perfect, you know — salvation is by grace". But this is the worst possible witness they could give! They should instead thank the person for revealing their fault to them, and never let it happen again. The non-Christians are looking to see if our actions match the bible, for even atheists know that Christians should "love their enemies" and "turn the other cheek".

We often spirtitualise the teaching of Jesus in the Sermon on the Mount, or water down the practical application of it, because we are afraid that we cannot live up to it. However, non-Christians are never satisfied with this; they quite rightly expect that Jesus said exactly what he meant to say.

Outward holiness is simply a matter of controlling our actions by strength of will. This is only what any non-Christian does, and there are very few people who do not put some sort of restraints on their old nature. For example, a businessman may desire to have a sexual relationship with every attractive secretary in his employment. He may restrain himself, not because his desires have become moral, but maybe because he is married, or he has his respectability to protect, or perhaps he has a fear of being rejected or criticised.

Another example might be a housewife who desires furniture or clothes that she could never afford. Her heart desires these things, and so she has covetousness in her heart, but she would never actually steal the things she desires, or defraud a shopping catalogue, for fear of the consequences and the condemnation of others. She stays respectable, but the condition in her heart stays the same — covetous. She has controlled her lustful desires, the nature she inherited from Adam, by strength of will.

Christians are not exempt

These examples could be multiplied dozens of times over to suit any circumstance. No Christian is exempt from these same desires. They are so common in our daily lives that they happen subconsciously; and Christians would be horrified if they had to give an account for their **desires** rather than their **actions**. We all tend to justify ourselves according to our actions, not according to our inner desires and lusts.

People who have a weak will succumb to their heart's desires, and so they either justify their action, or else they feel condemned and weak. But this is not the way forward for a Christian, because self-justification and condemnation are both wrong. The simple fact is that our will is not the root of our problem, and God always deals with roots and beginnings.

No action can take place without our mind being involved. **Thought** is always the root, the first thing, and only after we have exercised our mind does our will come into play, and we decide upon an outward course of action. We may succeed or fail in our action, depending on whether we are strong or weak-willed; but the root of the process is not our will, it is our thinking. I'm sure no-one will contest this obvious fact, but it is fundamental to our understanding of the process of holiness, because if we do not start at the very beginning, we will only end up in hyprocrisy. When our actions and thoughts do not agree, we deceive ourselves and the people who observe us.

Change your attitude

There is a maxim that I would recommend every Christian to engrave on their hearts: **If you cannot change your circumstances, change your attitude**. Attitudes are to do with our mind — the way that we think — and if we can deal with this, our circumstances are of no consequence.

In Romans 12:2 Paul clearly shows us how we can change our thinking: *Be not **conformed** to this world: but be **transformed** by the renewing of your mind.* To "be conformed" means to come in line with, or to be "squeezed into the mould".

The world system incessantly bombards our minds with its philosophy and thinking on every conceivable subject from fashion to politics, from birth control to our sexual orientation. All the media are at its disposal — huge advertising hoardings on the sides of our streets which are impossible to miss, television and radio, newspapers and periodicals for every hobby, lust or technical subject — all these confront our minds and values every day. These media messages automatically conform us to this world if we allow ourselves to be exposed to them.

No different

A general look at modern Christians will confirm this fact, for their style of dress, their home decor, their recreation and entertainment are no different from that of any other moral person in their own country. We watch the same adverts, see the same posters, read the same papers, and unfortunately we are influenced in the same way.

Renewing the mind

Paul shows us that the only way to counter this bombardment of our minds is also to do with the mind. He tells us that we are to be *transformed*, changed, by a process of renewal. This process, like the world's, also works by repetition. The world conforms us, often without our consent. I find advertising in public places distasteful and offensive because I have no choice as to whether I see the posters or not. I have no way to alter this situation, because I travel so much in large cities. I must see hundreds of posters every day just taking my two children to school. My children are also being conditioned by the images displayed on the posters, and I cannot alter this fact.

The repetitive messages of the adverts are a form of brainwashing, because it is without my consent. But **repetition by consent** is not brainwashing, but **renewing**

— that is, a constant, conscious change of mind which will eventually permeate through to our actions. This is the secret, because then our actions become unassuming, and our righteousness is no longer the self-righteousness that comes from our own efforts; we are no longer trying to conform our actions to a moral code of conduct.

Starting the process

I am convinced that if we can change our thinking, which means our attitudes, then we need do nothing more. We have started the process of holiness, and it will have its own results in due course. Romans 12 lists an amazing number of attitudes that we can adopt for ourselves. I have listed thirty such attitudes from just this chapter in the margin of my bible; but all the epistles are full of instruction as to what our attitudes should be towards our pastors, families, or work situations. Here are a few examples, which show us that these scriptures are telling us primarily how to **think**.

Don't think of yourself more highly than you ought to, but think soberly, according as God has given to every man the measure of faith.
Let love be sincere.
Be kind and affectionate to each other, in honour preferring one another.
Don't be lazy in your work.
Bless those that curse you.
Be of the same mind one toward another.
Don't be high minded, but come down to the level of men of low status.
Don't think too much of your own opinions.
Don't seek revenge for yourself.

These verses sound very much like the beatitudes. It is easy to think of humility or meekness as tangible "qualities" or characteristics of behaviour that we need to possess, but they are not. They are only attitudes — ways of thinking. Humility or meekness are not what we **do** (our actions), but ways of **thinking**, because humility and meekness are decisions, choices, in our minds.

The mind of Christ

If you read through the epistles you will be surprised to find many references to the mind, and Paul often uses Jesus as an example of how our thinking should be. In Philippians 2:1, Paul asks a question to which every Christian must answer yes. *Have you found any consolation in Christ, any comfort of love, any fellowship of the spirit, any bowels and mercies?* Paul knows that we have indeed found all these things in our Saviour, and so he can challenge us with his following statement in verse 2: *Please make me happy, by being **like-minded**, having the same love, being of one accord, of one mind.*

In verse 3 he then goes on to explain how we should think. It should not be done *with a motive of strife or worthless pride, but by **lowliness of mind** we should esteem others better than ourselves.* Verse 5 says, *Let **this mind** be in you that was also in Christ Jesus*; and then, lest we think it is unattainable, he helps us by telling us how Christ **thought**. It is revealing, for it shows us that true humility is an **attitude** — it's in the way we think. Verse 6 tells us that *Jesus **thought** it not robbery to be equal with God.* This is not the statement of a proud person, for in Jesus' life it was a simple fact, a true assessment. Verse 7 tells us that *he humbled himself even to the death of the cross.* Humbling yourself is a very different situation from allowing yourself to be humbled. A proud person could be humbled, but he would never willingly humble himself, because humbling yourself demands an attitude of humility, a way of thinking. Circumstances can humble a person, but circumstances can never change their way of thinking. They may be humbled or humiliated, but they can still remain proud in their hearts.

Think like Christ

We often ask God to change our circumstances, but God always requires a change of attitude in our minds before he can do this. In fact, often when we do change our attitudes, we find that are we actually quite content with our outward circumstances. This only goes to prove that the problem was not really in the circumstances, but in our attitude towards them.

If as Christians we can start to think as Christ thought and stop our minds being conditioned by the world's thinking, the process of holiness will begin. Let me stress again that it is a process, and a lifetime's commitment; but no-one has an excuse not to **start** this process.

Chapter 16

Cause and Effect

The righteousness of God is revealed from faith to faith: as it is written, the just shall live by faith. For the wrath of God is revealed from heaven against all ungodleness and unrighteousness of men, who hold the truth in unrighteousness; because that which may be known of God is manifest in them; for God has shown it unto them. For the invisible things of him from the creation of the world are clearly seen, being understood by the things that are made, even his eternal power and Godhead; so that they are without excuse.

Romans 1:17-20

Paul tells us in the above verses that God's wrath against ungodly men will be completely justified. No-one will have an excuse, because God's laws in his creation reveal his character. This is true of any personality. We all reveal our characters by the way we decorate our homes, the way we clothe ourselves and by our general lifestyles. I am not calling these laws "laws of science", for in reality there is no such thing.

Science only discovers laws that already exist in God's creation. There is no distinction between so-called "natural laws" of maths, chemistry and physics, and spiritual laws. There is no "natural science" or "nature". The world was created **supernaturally**. Creation is an act of God, not a progression or evolution. It is humanistic thinking to attribute everything to natural causes.

All laws of creation are spiritual

Why, as Christians, is it important to understand this principle? I will explain. If we think that a "law of science" is only a natural law and nothing to do with God's character, then we will not apply it to our spiritual life, and we will miss so many insights, instructions and directions that affect our daily lives. We will have to revert to man-derived doctrines of humanistic thinking for instructions in our daily lifestyles.

Allow me to take a simple law that everyone learns at school — the law of "cause and effect". We accept that there can be no effect without there first being a cause. If we realise that this is a spiritual law then we can apply it to our pursuit of holiness.

The effect

As Christians our desire is to be holy. This is the **effect** we desire. Causes are different from effects. The priniciple is that in order to obtain the effect, you only need the cause; you seek the cause, not the effect. The effect will be a natural consequence of the cause. Therefore, the last thing we should do is try to be holy ourselves. All we need do is seek the **cause** of holiness.

Trying to be holy can never make us holy. It can only make us hypocrites. For if we assume we have reached our aim by achieving an outward holiness, all we have really achieved is a pseudo-effect without a cause, and this now becomes a lie, a masquerade, a pretence — which is a perfect definition of hypocrisy.

The cause

Many Christians try to be holy, and recognise that they fail. They are honest with themselves and admit that their outward actions do not match their inward attitudes; and this can only produce frustration and failure, for the simple reason that the fixed law of cause and effect says that we must go to the **cause** if we want the effect. Self can never change self. Therefore we should not strive for holiness, because it would become "self-holiness" — which is no better than self-righteousness. We need instead to seek the **cause** of holiness — the things that make us holy. This will bring a great freedom, because the things that cause us to be holy are things that we can do.

Frustrated Christians

Many Christians who try to be holy get frustrated and end up feeling that holiness is unachievable, that it consists of doing things which are impossible to do. But the cause of holiness consists of easily achievable things which we **can** do. They are not difficult to do if we want to do them.

The other great benefit in seeking the cause and not the effect is that our holiness now becomes a natural consequence, because our attention is focussed on the cause of holiness, not on holiness itself. The result is that we do become holy, but we are not aware of our holiness. There is nothing worse in a person than self-conscious holiness — every time they do something good or righteous, they are conscious of it: another holy deed, another holy act. They become so self-aware of their own holiness, that they and everyone else know it, and then it becomes simply a way of drawing attention to themselves. It is actually self-righteousness, and not righteousness by faith at all.

If we pursue the cause rather than the effect, our holiness is not self-conscious, it is unassuming. This is the only true holiness, the holiness that is hidden from ourselves. People then *see our good works* and glorify not us, but *our Father in heaven*; and this protects us from pride and self-righteousness.

God's glory

Let us look at 2 Corinthians 3:18, and see how this law of cause and effect applies to our pursuit of holiness. Paul says, *We all, with open face beholding in a glass the glory of the Lord, are changed into the same image from glory to glory, even as by the spirit of the Lord.*

There are key words in any text, and we need to understand them before the whole verse can be explained. Firstly I want to examine the word "glory". From childhood I have heard and read it thousands of times, and yet if asked to explain it I would have been embarrassed, because I never really understood it. I associated it with the *shekinah* in the tabernacle or some kind of holy light as depicted on a Greek icon. I have since learned that these things are only a **manifestation** of God's glory, and that "glory" itself can often be substituted by the word **character**. Glory is God's very essence and being.

To support this definition let us look at two scriptures that use this word. Moses in Exodus 33:18 said to God, *Show me your **glory**.* God hid Moses in the cleft of a rock and then declared his **character**: chapter 34:6-7. In the New Testament, in John 17, Jesus prayed to his Father and said, *I have **glorified** thee on the earth; I have finished the work that you gave me to do.* How did Jesus **glorify** God on the earth? Surely it was by revealing God's **character** to mankind.

If we substitute the word "character" in our text we will understand what Paul is inferring. *But we all, with open face beholding the **character** of the Lord, are changed into the same image from **character to character.***

Can it be so simple? Is it possible that by looking into God's character, we can be changed into the very same character? It seems far too simplistic. We have been used to striving in our wills to be holy, and it does not seem reasonable that it can happen without our great efforts. But let us not forget that Paul is not focussing on the **effects**, but the **cause**. He is showing us the roots of holiness.

Little by little

The second thing I want to look at in this scripture is the **process** which Paul is showing us, for he says *from glory to glory* — from character to character. This means that holiness does not come from a single act which yields an immediate reaction, but is a process which happens by degrees; little by little we *grow in grace*. An act can have immediate effects, but a process takes time; and holiness is a process. Therefore we should not expect quick or instant results. We should realise that our growth in holiness will be slow, and often not even recognisable because of the slow rate of growth. We have to look back over a period of time in order to see the progress; but the results will be sure, and we can be confident that if we are dealing with the cause, then the effects will take care of themselves. Holiness will actually become a natural part of us.

The mirror

The third and last word I want to examine is "glass", which means "mirror". Paul says that if we behold the character of the Lord *with open face* (that is, honestly, or with expectancy) *as in a glass,* we are changed into that same image.

Why would Paul use this expression? What happens when we look into a mirror? We see an image, a vision, a picture of what we are looking at. We must remember here that we are to look at the character of Christ as if it were an image, something we can visualise, something that becomes clear to our vision. When we see something pictorially, then we are no longer in any doubt as to its image.

Whatever comes out of us is only a reflection of what has already gone into us. Nothing at all can come out of our bodies and minds that didn't first go in. We are all products of our environments, that is to say of the outside influences which have gone into us over the course of our lives. Our dialects of speech and our cultural behaviour all reveal our outside influences. So to change our outward behaviour we first have to expose ourselves to other, different influences. These must be outside influences also, for we cannot change ourselves by ourselves; self can never change self.

Seeing and understanding

We should now begin to understand how the law of cause and effect can be used in our pursuit of holiness. If we can only look into the character of God and see clearly what it is, then the very image that comes into our consciousness will automatically be reflected out in our lives. It is impossible for it not to happen.

Our difficulty in holiness is therefore not in striving to be holy in our outward behaviour, but in seeing and understanding what is the true character of God. This is the sticking point, the point which so many Christians fail to understand in their pursuit of holiness.

We may also reverse the equation and say that people who are not outwardly holy are people who do not see clearly or understand the true character of God, or holiness.

Jesus our example

Jesus is our example of holiness. In John's gospel chapter 12:44-45, Jesus made a statement which shows us that he, too, only reflected his Father's character and not his own. He said, *He that believes on me, does not believe on me, but on him that sent me. And he that sees me, sees him that sent me.* Clearly, Jesus was saying that he was only a reflection of his Father in heaven. This is an exciting revelation, because it means that if we concentrate on our **influences** instead of on our **circumstances**, then we will automatically reflect those same influences in our own lives. It will be natural and easy.

If we honestly compare the amount of time most Christians spend being influenced by the world's system with the amount of time they spend being influenced by the kingdom of God, the results are embarrassing. Take, for example, the time spent in reading technical, fashion, news, and entertainment literature, compared with the time spent reading God's word. Most people would have to admit that the time spent reading God's word was only a fraction of time spent reading other literature. Our principle of cause and effect tells us that we can and will only reflect this balance of influences in our daily lives and outward behaviour.

Influences

The media now play a vital and pivotal role in our world systems, not only in entertainment but politics, commerce and religion. The propaganda machinery is frightening in its power and influence. A whole planet is being slowly conditioned to accept lifestyles and ways of thinking in a way that would have been impossible only 70 years ago.

On the issue of homosexuality, for example: 70 years ago homosexuality was looked upon by virtually all of society as a wicked perversion. But if you now ask a 60 or 70-year-old what they think about homosexuality, they would be far more likely to say that we have to be tolerant and open-minded, and that some people are born with homosexual leanings, and it is a part of our genetic programming. My point is not whether this tolerance is good or bad, but that slowly a change has taken place, and it has happened on an unprecedented world-wide scale because of the influence of the media.

Our only reference

If we want to know the character of God, the bible is our only place of reference, and we neglect it at our peril. Books on doctrine and theology are no substitute for the simple word of God. Sermons, which are very necessary for us, are still no substitute for spending time alone with God. A personal relationship has to be developed on a one-to-one basis, and this can never happen in public meetings or when other people are around.

If we will only look into the perfect character of God and his holiness, then the outward life will be affected in due course, and it will be a holiness without hypocrisy, because it will be a reflection, not of our efforts, but of the very life of Christ.

If there was one part of the bible that epitomises the character of God for a modern disciple it is the Sermon on the Mount in Matthew chapters 5, 6 and 7. I believe that all the letters to the churches from Paul, Peter, James, John and Jude only paraphrase and amplify the Sermon on the Mount. I also am convinced that all the law and the prophets are embraced and fulfilled in this profound teaching of Jesus to his disciples.

A personal postscript

The next book in this series on **Radical Christianity** will begin a study of this marvellous teaching from the master teacher himself. It has revolutionised my own life through the principle we have looked at of cause and effect. As I realised this principle, and began to practise the cause of holiness instead of the effect, subjecting myself to the influence of God's character as much as I could by reading the bible, praying, fasting and spending time alone with God, I found that I began to change outwardly despite myself. The changes I saw in myself often surprised me, because I wasn't trying to be holy any more. I'd stopped trying to be holy, and yet I was achieving the effect I had so long desired — becoming holy.

I am talking about a period of over twenty years, and so I am speaking from experience when I say that this is a process which cannot be obtained instantly, or even over a short period of time. Patience and perseverance are all part of the process.

I am convinced that the failure of many Christians is that they never get around to **beginning** this process. May I challenge everyone who reads this book to saturate themselves with the Sermon on the Mount until it begins to work out practically in their own lives.

Turn your eyes upon Jesus
Look full in his wonderful face
And the things of earth will grow strangely dim
In the light of his glory and grace

Maurice Barratt

Maurice Barratt was brought up under the dynamic Pentecostal ministry of his father Bill Barratt, part of the Barratt and Williams healing ministry in the 1950s and 60s.

He became a Christian at the age of six, and from his youth lived a conventional charismatic Christian lifestyle. But at the age of 30 he was deeply affected by his father's teaching from the Sermon on the Mount on the principles of real Christian discipleship — what it really means to follow Jesus. From that time on he began to change from a conventional, "normal" Christian to a man convinced that what is lacking in Christians today is not supernatural power or gifts but the fruit, the character of Christ.

For the last twenty years Maurice has been committed to his call — to teach the church the practical principles of discipleship. He has taught in churches, housegroups, prisons, schools and bible colleges, throughout Europe and the USA.

Many of Maurice's messages are recorded on cassette, including a major series on the Sermon on the Mount covering 55 cassettes, and messages on many other subjects concerning Christian life and conduct.

Maurice Barratt is available for ministry and can be contacted at the address opposite.

About Barratt Ministries

Barratt Ministries is a Manchester-based Christian organization founded in 1985. Directors Maurice and Joanna Barratt have an international preaching and teaching ministry. Joanna is a singer with 9 music albums of her own songs, including two major projects of scripture in song — Psalm 119 and The Sermon on the Mount. Joanna also ministers in prisons and women's fellowships.

Barratt Ministries is a multi-media ministry, involved in the publication of books and literature, the recording of music albums and teaching cassettes, production of videos and programmes for Christian radio.

Barratt Ministries publishes *Challenge*, a newsletter with teaching articles by Maurice and Joanna Barratt, every two months. It is available free of charge and post-free on request.

For a full list of Barratt Ministries publications please contact:

Barratt Ministries
114 Daisy Bank Road
Victoria Park
Manchester M14 5QH
England
Tel & Fax: +44 (0)161 224 2620
E-mail: bminmcr@aol.com

Also available from Barratt Ministries Publications:

Playing With Fire

the use and abuse of music

by Alex Robertson

MUSIC IS POWER ... power to influence and inspire, or to manipulate and control. It can be a wonderful means of expression, or a potent and addictive drug.
Playing With Fire is about the use and abuse of that power. Christians today stand at a crossroads with regard to music. Some welcome joyfully the arrival of new styles and sounds into Christian worship. Others feel that the church is compromising with the world. Many are just confused. There are important questions which demand answers:

Why does music affect us so powerfully?

What is God's purpose for music?

What makes the difference between the use and abuse of music?

This wide-ranging and stimulating book deals with these and many other issues. Written by a professional musician, *Playing With Fire* explodes the myths, explores the roots and explains the facts about music. This is a book to provoke thought, prayer and change.

***Alex Robertson** read music at Cambridge University and studied at the Royal Northern College of Music in Manchester. He has been a member of Barratt Ministries since 1985.*

Published by Barratt Ministries Publications
240 pages ISBN 0 9528222 0 2